100 IDEAS
FOR TEACHING CITIZENSHIP

D1310172

CONTINUUM ONE HUNDREDS SERIES

100 IDEAS
FOR TEACHING
CITIZENSHIP

Ian Davies

continuum
LONDON • NEW YORK

To Lynn, Hannah, Matthew and Rachael

Continuum International Publishing Group

The Tower Building   15 East 26th Street
11 York Road   New York
London   NY 10010
SE1 7NX

www.continuumbooks.com

British Library Cataloguing-in-Publication Data

A catalogue record for this book is available from the British
Library.

ISBN: 0–8264–8494–8 (paperback)

Designed and typeset by Ben Cracknell Studios | Janice Mather

Printed and bound in Great Britain by MPG Books Ltd, Bodmin

CONTENTS

SECTION 3 **Teaching citizenship**

SECTION 4 **Developing students' skills**

SECTION 5 **Whole-school approaches**

SECTION 6 Running a school council

SECTION 7 Setting up a mock election

SECTION 8 Citizenship lessons

SECTION 9 **Assessing students?**

SECTION 10 **Government departments, offices and agencies**

SECTION 11 **Examination syllabuses**

SECTION 12 **Learning from others**

SECTION 13 **Professional development**

This short book is not designed to provide all the answers that anyone needs to be the perfect teacher of citizenship. Citizenship and citizenship education are too controversial, contested and perhaps confusing for anyone to be able to make such a sweeping claim.

It is right and proper that those involved in citizenship education should engage in a healthy and lively debate that is itself an indication of a democratic pluralistic society. There should never be one form of citizenship education, but there can be greater clarity about the key issues that characterize those forms. Here there are activities that can be valued and enjoyed by learners. When factual information has been included my intention is to encourage teachers to promote the skills associated with citizenship. Information from all sources needs to be considered critically as we explore concepts and issues as they arise in public contexts.

When I have given ideas for citizenship education through other subjects (such as history) I want the focus to remain clearly on the essentials of citizenship. I hope there'll be an integrated approach to knowledge and skills so that young people can learn to think and act through their exploration of social and political issues in a modern multi-faith liberal democracy.

This book will be good for a positive, creative and democratic form of citizenship education if teachers and others are sufficiently stimulated, in a constructively critical manner, to try out some of the ideas and then develop their own.

Ian Davies

What you need to know . . .

CITIZENSHIP

In *Citizenship and Social Class*, T. H. Marshall suggested during the eighteenth century property rights had been recognized and so led to a form of civil citizenship; in the nineteenth century, as more people were allowed to vote, political rights grew; and in the twentieth century welfare developed, showing that social rights are important. Not everyone accepts Marshall's ideas but much of current educational policy (including the National Curriculum for Citizenship) emerges at least in part from his characterization of citizenship.

There are two competing traditions associated with citizenship: the liberal (rights based) and the civic republican (based around notions of duties or responsibilities). Increasingly, reference is made to a possible third tradition that is to do with communitarianism. There are other vitally important characterizations of citizenship that, for example, emphasize identity.

Questions that can be considered in relation to rights and duties include: Is there too much freedom for young people today? Should I be forced to keep the law even if it is not just? Should I give to charitable causes? And so on. Some claim that rights and duties are ultimately hard to distinguish (is it my right or duty, as a parent, to look after my children?) but even so, it may be worth using these labels as a way of helping students to understand debates about issues in society today.

The National Curriculum for Citizenship looks to develop knowledge and understanding through the development of skills of enquiry and communication and participation and responsible action (this is very different from an approach that might recommend the teaching of knowledge as something that is more important, and separate from, forms of involvement).

Key reading:
Heater, D. (1999) *What is Citizenship?* Cambridge: Polity Press.
T.H.Marshall (1963) 'Citizenship and Social Class', *in Sociology at the Crossroads and other essays.* London: Heinemann.

For students to engage in debates and other activities they should have relevant knowledge. Depending on the educational purpose of the activity being studied, it's useful to know the basics of local government (role of councillors and the extent of their decision-making power), national government (the system of elections, role of an MP, role of ministers), the role of international organizations (G8, United Nations, European Union) and the key issues that dominate the UK and the world (currently, for example, terrorism, the environment, discrimination and prejudice, North–South).

Four key areas are:

o political concepts (e.g. power, authority, justice);
o political institutions (elected and nominated);
o issues (either generally phrased, for example, terrorism; or connected more directly to specific events or contexts, for example, the issue of iraq);
o political skills and dispositions appropriate for a democracy (making a case, discussion, debate about political issues).

One idea to try out:

What qualities should a politician have? Diamond-rank a series of qualities (skills/characteristics/attributes) and ask small groups of students to justify their decisions. Diamond ranking means ordering statements to show the perceived relative importance, or significance, with the first 'X' the most important and the bottom 'X' the least important, for example:

X
XX
XXX
XX
X

Statements, written on slips of paper, could be: honesty; good public speaker; intelligent; healthy; hard working; looks good on TV; able to write so that many people understand; good organizer; strong personal beliefs.

This allows students to debate and discuss while shifting the statements easily as the discussion develops. This activity allows students to reach clear conclusions but emphasizes the process of active discussion. It can be adapted for many other questions. For example, if asking 'what is a democracy?' – and wanting to emphasize that there are many different types of democracy – the nine statements could be: voting for the government by adults; free press; rule of law; equal opportunities; high standards of living; active charities; education for all young people; full employment; involvement with international organizations like the UN.

Key reading (with lots of activities for teaching):
Huddleston, T. (2004) *Citizens and Society: political literacy teacher resource pack*. London: Hodder and Stoughton.

The creation and distribution of wealth is centrally relevant to citizenship as it tells us about issues of power, equality and justice. There are masses of resources available for those who wish to develop the economic aspects of citizenship. The Economics and Business Studies Association is a good contact and most LEAs have a business education partnership team. Resources have been developed by the Institute for Citizenship (www.citizen.org) and there are three briefing papers about economics and citizenship on the citizEd project website (www.citized.info). Many resources for schools are available at www.pfeg.org.uk.

There are a number of routes into this issue. For example, students may want to know what they can do when they save or spend money. A number of very simple exercises to do with decisions about pocket money can be set up. A survey of how much people in the class earn could be undertaken (if managed very sensitively) or, if that's too problematic, the class could be asked how much they think they should be paid by their parents/guardians. Ideas about money paid in exchange for 'services', annual increases, relative and absolute wealth and taxation normally come quickly into the discussion.

Another exercise to do with personal finance relates to shopping. Ask your students to imagine they've bought a faulty product or they want to exchange something. What they'd like to do with the product and what they can legally expect can be discussed. These matters can be explored by using simple legal guides about personal finance (see www.citizen.org.uk/education/resources/economic.pdf). The government's views about financial literacy for school students can be seen at www.dfes.gov.uk/publications/guidanceonthelaw/fcg/KS3&4.pdf.

Young enterprise schemes (www.young-enterprise.org.uk) help students think about issues to do with work, profit and loss. It might be useful to explore some ethical issues, especially in international contexts. For example, a debate about the ways in which schools responded in 2005 to the Asian tsunami crisis could be interesting. Students can have a go at running the economy if they go to the game at www.bized.ac.uk.

The law, and whether or not the law is the same thing as justice, is one of the most fundamental aspects of citizenship education. Many organizations exist to bring the law to life. Mock trials can be conducted and perhaps the best-known service for this purpose in the UK is the Bar National Mock Trail Competition (see www.lawreports.co.uk/BarNatMkTr.htm). A historical example of a mock trial – exploring the Amistad case – can be seen at: http://projects.edtech.sandi.net/hoover/amistad/. At times some distinctions are made between mock trials and the running of a moot (see www.lse.ac.uk/collections/LSEMooting Department/essentials.htm).

A visit to a magistrates' court is a valuable experience and I've found there's a definite commitment to education on the part of magistrates. A visit needs to be carefully handled: it can be voyeuristic; individuals known to the young people might be involved; the seating arrangements can make it difficult for all to hear what's going on; there can be a lot of administrative and technical material to deal with; and there will be unexpected developments such as last minute cancellations.

It might be more appropriate on occasion simply to examine real or imaginary cases in the classroom or to invite in a magistrate who's a good communicator with young people. For guidelines from another context on inviting speakers to school, see the following from the DfES: 'Making the most of visitors: using outside agencies in school drug education'. The Advisory Council for Alcohol and Drug Education/London Drugs Policy Forum International resources can be used both in their own right and also to develop comparative understanding (e.g. an example of a US based organization can be seen at www.clrep.org/).

There is no simple answer to the question of the overlaps and distinctions between law and justice, but reminding students of the issues is a great way for them to focus on the activities.

The previous ideas (law, economics, etc.) are given concrete expression in real world contexts by institutions such as the World Trade Organization (WTO). It was established in 1995 and is based in Geneva, Switzerland. It makes rules about international trade and aims to increase incomes and promote peace through trade. The WTO has 147 member-countries (on 23 April 2004) who discuss and agree on such things as tariffs; a budget of 169 million Swiss francs (in 2005); and a staff of 600 people. The WTO has a number of functions including providing a forum for trade negotiations and handling trade disputes.

Detailed reporting on disputes can be seen on the WTO website (http://www.wto.org/index.htm).

A class exercise on sugar subsidies can be set up. For example, there is the following statement about sugar at www.bbc.co.uk/schools/citizenx/internat/global/lowdown/trade_info_1.shtml.

○ Sugar prices are protected by tariffs and quotas in the EU, Japan and US. Producers in these countries receive about double the world market price for the sugar they grow.
○ Producers in the richer countries are subsidised at US$6.4 billion per year, an amount nearly equal to ALL developing country exports.
○ These subsidies encourage people to grow sugar beet in cold countries and for sugar processors to reduce the amount of sugar they import from cane-producing countries such as the West Indies.

Start a lesson by sharing some sweets, asking about the price and suggesting that each person would in the near future have to pay three times the current price. Suggest that this price rise was due to a determination to address the situation described above about subsidies for sugar. Some research would be needed using data from the websites shown above as well as current media reports. Students could then be asked to present three points for and against the removal of subsidies from countries that are from the richer north of the world.

THE WORLD TRADE ORGANIZATION

THE UNITED NATIONS

The basic facts about the United Nations (UN) are described very clearly at the following: www.un.org/ aboutun/basicfacts/index.html.

In brief, the UN was set up in 1945 and began with a membership of 50 countries. Its purpose is

> to maintain international peace and security; to develop friendly relations among nations; to cooperate in solving international economic, social, cultural and humanitarian problems and in promoting respect for human rights and fundamental freedoms; and to be a centre for harmonizing the actions of nations in attaining these ends.

There are a number of key structures including the General Assembly, the International Court of Justice and the Security Council. The UN is not a world government and relies on support from members, especially those who belong to the Security Council.

There is a United Nations Association for the UK and its website includes information about study tours and other activities (see www.una-uk.org/citizenship/ teachingtheun.html).

Teachers can include issues about the United Nations by establishing or becoming involved in a Model United Nations activity. Detailed guidance about how to proceed can be seen at www.munga-una.org.uk/.

The G8 is described at www.g7.utoronto.ca/what_is_g8. html. Since 1975, the heads of state or government of the major industrial democracies have been meeting annually at a summit to deal with the major economic and political issues facing their domestic societies and the international community as a whole. The current members are France, the US, the UK, Germany, Japan, Italy, Canada, the European Community and Russia. Each summit deals with macroeconomic management, international trade, and relations with developing countries as well as many other matters including energy, terrorism, crime, etc.

In addition to the main summit there are supporting ministerial meetings. The summit sets priorities, defines new issues and provides guidance to established international organizations. The annual meeting has been an opportunity for anti-globalization demonstrations since the Birmingham Summit in 1998 and the protests turned violent in 2001 at the Genoa Summit, resulting in the death of a protestor.

There is detailed information about the workings of the G8 at various websites. The following is a site based at the University of Toronto and gives links to many other agencies: www.g7.utoronto.ca.

For older and more academically able students opportunities exist to consider the extent countries actually meet their commitments given at previous summits. An interesting report about compliance can be seen at: http://www.g7.utoronto.ca/evaluations/2003evian _comp_final/01-2003_final_intro.pdf. Students could be asked to develop a list of reasons (going beyond a simple identification of greed) that might explain why the promises made by politicians are not always kept. Ask students to talk about this in pairs and then to share their reasoning in small groups. This could then lead to full class discussions.

Or, there are many opportunities to review media reports about current or previous G8 summits. Some fairly simple questions could be posed about what the summit did, but perhaps also a more focused question could explore the actions of the protestors and the responses from

the politicians. The summits are being held in increasingly
isolated locations. Do students think there's a need for this
(for the safety of those who might protest and to ensure a
secure environment) or do they feel that decisions should
be made from public spaces? The question could be: 'is it
acceptable for a G8 summit to be held in an isolated
location that is heavily guarded?'

Full information about the European Union (EU) can be seen at www.europa.eu.int/index_en.htm but briefly, there are five EU institutions, each playing a specific role:

o European Parliament (elected by the peoples of the Member States);
o Council of the European Union (representing the governments of the Member States);
o European Commission (driving force and executive body);
o Court of Justice (ensuring compliance with the law);
o Court of Auditors (controlling sound and lawful management of the EU budget).

These are backed up by other important bodies, including the European Economic and Social Committee (expresses the opinions of organized civil society on economic and social issues) and the European Central Bank (responsible for monetary policy and managing the euro).

Initially, the EU consisted of six countries: Belgium, Germany, France, Italy, Luxembourg and the Netherlands. Denmark, Ireland and the UK joined in 1973; Greece in 1981; Spain and Portugal in 1986; and Austria, Finland and Sweden in 1995. In 2004 the biggest ever enlargement took place with ten new countries joining. An interesting class debate could involve discussing benefits/weaknesses of enlarging the EU.

Various resources about European citizenship suitable for both teachers and students can be seen at: http://europa.eu.int/youth/active_citizenship/index_eu_en.html.

There are many activities that could be suggested about the EU, some of which are very ambitious and time consuming, for example taking part in one of the study tours or cross-national projects funded by the EU, such as Comenius in which schools join together to work on specific issues. However, a fairly brief exercise could focus around whether the UK should join the euro. A debate could be established following preparation in which there are three parties: the 'Euro party' who want to join immediately; the 'Wait and See party' and the 'Keep us Out of the Euro party'. Each party should make a two-minute statement with questions and discussion around economics and politics (including personal and national identity).

The *Observer* newspaper carried a full outline of the debates about the euro on 18 February 2001. This information would be of great use for students undertaking research for the debate. Back copies of newspapers are normally available through most public libraries or the newspaper's website.

A variety of organizations, besides the EU, exist that are absolutely fundamental to an understanding of Europeanism. Perhaps the most significant is the Council of Europe. Below is a brief summary of the work of the Council of Europe which has been summarized from the official website (www.coe.int).

The Council of Europe was founded in 1949 and is based in Strasbourg. It groups together 46 countries, including 21 countries from Central and Eastern Europe. The Council was set up to:

1   defend human rights, parliamentary democracy and the rule of law;
2   develop continent-wide agreements to standardize member countries' social and legal practices;
3   promote awareness of a European identity based on shared values and cutting across different cultures.

There are two main component parts of the Council of Europe. First, the Committee of Ministers is composed of the 46 foreign ministers or their Strasbourg-based deputies (ambassadors/permanent representatives) and is the organization's decision-making body. Second, the Parliamentary Assembly groups 630 members (315 representatives and 315 substitutes) from the 46 national parliaments and any Special Guest Delegations from candidate countries.

The Council of Europe has newsletters, courses and conferences that are targeted at teachers. A teaching idea can be easily developed. Imagine that Libya has applied to become a member of the Council of Europe. Ask your class to investigate the request (see http://europa.eu.int/comm/external_relations/) using the following categories.

o   Geography: Libya is part of Africa not Europe (but it's closer to some European capitals than parts of the UK; Russia is a member of the Council of Europe).
o   Culture: Christianity is a strong influence in the heritage of Europe but is it acceptable to exclude a state on the basis of its religion? In any case there are increasing numbers of people who are not Christians who are European.

o Politics: Libya doesn't have a good record on human rights but the UK and other countries have recently made positive moves towards Libya and there are states that are already part of the Council of Europe that have been taken to the European Court of Human Rights and lost (including the UK).

By examining the responses to these questions can we clarify the nature of what it means to be European?

In 1992 the United Nations (UN) held an Earth Summit in Rio de Janeiro, Brazil, where Agenda 21 was adopted by 178 governments. In 1999 the UK produced its own plan for how it would help achieve the goals of Agenda 21 (www.sustainable-development.gov.uk/what/what.htm). There is a DfES scheme of work that relates to Agenda 21 (www.standards.dfes.gov.uk/schemes2/ks4citizenship/cit12/12q3?view=get) and there are many other official and unofficial sites (e.g. www.scream.co.uk/?la21/). Many LEAs publicize their own work on their websites; the Geographical Association and the Royal Geographical Society produce their own material; and individual schools have reported on what they've done (e.g. www.la21.org.uk/).

In 2004 the Democracy through Citizenship project (part of the Institute for Citizenship) organized an event in which students from schools from six different LEAs came together to present the results of their research on climate change, recycling, waste management and to pose questions to an invited panel of politicians and environmentalists. Less ambitious work could take place by a class investigating the transport preferences and practices of teachers and students when travelling to and from school. Ask students to develop and then present proposals to improve transport and ask those reading or listening to those proposals to evaluate them on the basis of criteria such as cost, likely popularity and positive impact on the environment.

Alternatively, exploration could take place into a local controversial issue. For example, the City of York has recently introduced new parking charges. This led to strong and diverse ranges of reactions. The students could ask: Why was it done? What's the nature of the reactions – who's objecting, who's supportive? What alternatives there are? What might happen in the future? This could be achieved through several channels by:

o inviting different speakers into the classroom;
o reviewing newspaper reports;
o interviewing residents (or class members) about their views.

Organizations

The Citizenship Foundation aims to empower individuals to engage in the wider community through education about the law, democracy and society. We focus particularly on developing young people's citizenship skills, knowledge and understanding.

THE CITIZENSHIP FOUNDATION

The Citizenship Foundation, Ferroners House, Shaftesbury Place, Aldersgate Street, London EC2Y 8AA

Tel: 020 7367 0500
Fax: 020 7367 0501
Email: info@citizenshipfoundation.org.uk

The Citizenship Foundation (CF) began life as the Law in Education project and so it's not surprising that legal matters are still represented in the work of the charity. Activities for teachers include First Friday – seminars which take place on the first Friday of most months. The CF website carries details of a mock trial competition, a young person's passport (which explains many issues and is now in its ninth edition), a national youth parliament competition, as well as many other events and publications.

Valuable and practical classroom resources are also produced. Ted Huddleston, Don Rowe and Tony Thorpe are some of the people associated with the Foundation who write good classroom resources.

Key reading:
Thorpe, T. (2001) *Understanding Citizenship.* London: Hodder and Stoughton and the Citizenship Foundation.

ACT is the professional subject association for those involved in citizenship education. Our main aim is the furtherance of mutual support knowledge and good practice skills and resources for the teaching and learning of citizenship in schools and colleges.

ACT, Ferroners House, Shaftesbury Place,
Aldersgate Street, London EC2Y 8AA

Tel: 020 7367 0510
Email: info@teachingcitizenship.org.uk
www.teachingcitizenship.org.uk

ACT is an umbrella organization that emerged from close collaboration between a number of existing organizations involved in citizenship education (such as the Citizenship Foundation and the Institute for Citizenship). It came into being as citizenship education was introduced into the National Curriculum to support teachers. It provides:

o a magazine (*Teaching Citizenship*);
o an annual conference;
o a twice term electronic newsletter;
o interesting lesson plans;
o links to useful resources, such as training courses, assessment for citizenship and conferences.

Its founding president is Professor Sir Bernard Crick. It is closely associated with citizED (see www.citized. info), a project funded by the TTA that aims to help in the development of citizenship education teachers. The professional officer at the time of writing is Chris Waller who is (among many other things) setting up regional meetings of teachers and organizations, which are incredibly useful for teachers.

ASSOCIATION FOR CITIZENSHIP TEACHING (ACT)

IDEA

13

The Institute for Citizenship is an independent charitable trust. Our aim is to promote informed active citizenship and greater participation in democracy and society through a combination of community projects, research, education and discussion and debate.

Institute for Citizenship, Crown House, 51–52 Aldwych, London WC2B 4AX

Tel: 020 7844 5444
Email: info@citizen.org.uk
www.citizen.org.uk

A wide range of resources has been produced (see www.citizen.org.uk/education/resources.html). Some of these resources are available for free, others have been produced in association with commercial publishers such as Nelson Thornes (www.nelsonthornes.com). The textbooks by Lee Jerome and resources by Jeremy Hayward (based at the London Institute of Education) are very valuable. A great project managed by the Institute, and funded by the Joseph Rowntree Reform Trust, has taken place recently. It was based around community and schools and has been led in York by Bernie Flanagan and Jennifer Philpott.

Bernie is a community and youth worker and Jennifer is the citizenship consultant for the City of York LEA. They brought together young people from schools to influence local political systems.

INSTITUTE FOR CITIZENSHIP

Development education aims to raise awareness and understanding of how global issues affect the everyday lives of individuals, communities and societies and how all of us can and do influence the global.

The Development Education Association
33 Corsham Street, London N1 6DR

Tel: 020 7490 8108
Fax: 020 7490 8123
Email: dea@dea.org.uk/
www.dea.org.uk

An important perspective on citizenship is provided by the Development Education Association (DEA) including, but taking us beyond, issues to do with legal status in national contexts and exploring matters from various countries to promote skills and dispositions.

Various practical ways forward are possible. There are staff in Development Education Centres in different parts of the country working with local secondary teachers on how to introduce global citizenship into their schools. There is a free national magazine for secondary schools on global issues; a Spanish language television series for secondary pupils on the lives and views of young people from the UK, Spain, Western Sahara and Guatemala; and INSET training for teachers of post-16 students on bringing a global perspective to their work.

THE DEVELOPMENT EDUCATION ASSOCIATION

HANSARD SOCIETY

The Hansard Society is an independent, non-partisan educational charity which exists to promote effective parliamentary democracy. Good government needs to be supported and balanced by a strong, effective parliamentary democracy. Our work aims to strengthen parliament by encouraging greater accessibility and closer engagement with the public.

Hansard Society, LSE, 9 Kingsway,
London WC2B 6XF

Tel: 020 7395 4000
Fax: 020 7395 4008
hansard@hansard.lse.ac.uk
www.hansard-society.org.uk

The Hansard Society has been associated with research and development of citizenship education for a number of decades. It funded a very important piece of work in the 1970s to do with political education in which Bernard Crick was a key figure. This work influenced David Blunkett who would later become the Education Secretary of State and would introduce citizenship education into the National Curriculum. It is currently promoting the 'heads up' initiative (www.headsup.org.uk) which seeks to promote debate about contemporary issues among young people.

Other initiatives include consideration of e-democracy and how electronic voting, 'blogging' and other matters are affecting the nature of democracy. Its website is normally up to date with emerging issues and it encourages ways to listen to, and make links with, politicians.

Oxfam, Oxfam House, 274 Banbury Rd,
Oxford OX2 7DZ

Tel: 0870 333 2700
www.oxfam.org.uk

Below is a brief summary of the work of Oxfam which has been summarized from the official website.

Oxfam's beliefs are:

o The lives of all human beings are of equal value.
o In a world rich in resources, poverty is an injustice that must be overcome.
o Poverty makes people more vulnerable to conflict and natural calamity; much of this suffering can be prevented, and must be relieved.
o People's vulnerability to poverty and suffering is increased by unequal power relations based on, for example, gender, race, class, caste and disability; women, who make up a majority of the world's poor, are especially disadvantaged.
o Working together we can build a just and safer world, in which people take control over their own lives and enjoy their basic rights.
o To overcome poverty and suffering involves changing unjust policies and practices, nationally and internationally, as well as working closely with people in poverty.

Oxfam's identity:

o Oxfam works internationally as part of a world-wide movement to build a just and safer world.
o Oxfam is an independent British organization, registered as a charity, affiliated to Oxfam International, with partners, volunteers, supporters and staff of many nationalities.
o Oxfam is accountable both to those who support it and to those whom it seeks to benefit by its efforts.

The Carnegie UK Trust is an independent, not-for-profit foundation. We support research, public policy analysis and grass roots social action initiatives. Our work is non-partisan and dedicated to achieving practical results in people's lives.

CARNEGIE FOUNDATION

The Carnegie Foundation is based in the USA (www. carnegiefoundation.org), but the UK base of the Foundation can be discovered at www.carnegieuktrust. org.uk/.

It is interested in:

○ encouraging organizations to be more participatory;
○ identifying and promoting the benefits of young people's participation;
○ sharing good practice and improving opportunities for participation.

The Carnegie Foundation funds research and works in practical ways with schools and young people in other settings. It is possible for teachers to become involved in their initiatives and I would really recommend visiting their website.

The Politics Association welcomes the current impetus for citizenship education recognizing that citizenship is not watered down politics but has three essential elements – social and moral responsibility, community involvement and political literacy. The Association has significant experience in relation to the latter and has a real contribution to make to this tier of citizenship. It is active in producing specific material for classroom use, while seeking to set up partnerships with other organizations working for citizenship education which have experience of the other two tiers.

Politics Association, Old Hall Lane,
Manchester M13 0XT

Tel: 0161 256 3906
Fax: 0161 256 3906
Email: politic@enablis.co.uk
www.politicsassociation.com

The Politics Association publishes a magazine for teachers and students, *Talking Politics*, and runs an annual conference and events for school students. It is also active in collaboration with commercial publishers in the production of resources specifically targeted at citizenship education, but perhaps principally at students and teachers of examination courses in politics. It occupies a centrally important position in the history of the development of citizenship education. Individuals such as Bernard Crick and Derek Heater were key figures from its inception in 1969.

Key reading:
Crick, B. (2000) *Essays on Citizenship*. London: Continuum.

Association for the Teaching of Social Sciences
P.O. Box 6079, Leicester LE2 4DW

Tel: 0161 248 9375
Email: atss@btconnect.com
www.le.ac.uk/education/centres/ATSS/atss.html

ASSOCIATION FOR THE TEACHING
OF THE SOCIAL SCIENCES (ATSS)

The Association for the Teaching of Social Sciences, (ATSS) is a voluntary group of social science teachers. Composed of many sociologists, the ATSS also includes teachers of psychology, politics and economics among its members. The Association has close links with similar organizations such as the British Sociological Association, the Association of Psychology Teachers, the Politics Association and the Economics and Business Education Association.

The aim of the Association is to encourage and promote the teaching of social sciences in primary, secondary and higher education. It provides opportunities for those teaching in the social sciences to develop and share ideas and strategies for the promotion and delivery of their teaching. One of the main activities of the ATSS is the dissemination of information relating to teaching materials and teaching methods. The Association is also active in promoting the interests of social science teachers to examination boards, academic bodies, governmental and political agencies and the wider public.

Members receive:

1 Three copies per year of the journal *Social Science Teacher*.
2 An annual national conference for teachers and lecturers in the social sciences.
3 A regular newsletter.
4 A range of regional staff and student conferences.

School Councils UK is an educational charity which is recognized as Britain's most experienced training and support agency in the area of school and class councils. It has been helping schools to develop into caring communities working with teachers and pupils in primary, secondary and special schools for over ten years. School Councils UK developed out of successful adult and youth councils created by the charity Priority Area Development (PAD) in some of the most deprived neighbourhoods in Liverpool.

School Councils UK, 3rd Floor,
108–110 Camden High Street, London NW1 0LU

Tel: 0845 456 9428 (local call)
Fax: 0845 456 9429
www.schoolcouncils.org.uk

School councils, as shown later in this book (see Section 6), are a good way to promote active involvement by students. This charity provides a great background as to how school councils can be used to excellent effect in schools. School councils play a key role in the development of citizenship education.

SCHOOL COUNCILS UK

27

Teaching citizenship

HISTORY

There are many who have asserted that the connections between history and citizenship are very strong. For example, Derek Heater has argued that 'politics is present history; history is past politics'. Sample discussions and examples of classroom activities can be seen in Arthur *et al.* (2001). To explore the link between the two subjects there should be a recognizable citizenship element that reveals itself through a link between the past and contemporary society.

Get students looking at features of the past that are part of our contemporary society and work on what they reveal about our ideas today. Organize a thought shower, or present a list of special days that are commemorated, place names and symbols. Research their origins and suggest their current meanings. Waterloo station, Trafalgar Square, 'Land of hope and glory' and the Union Jack could be included as well as others such as United Nations Day, the flag of the European Union and the right to vote for 18-year-olds.

Two key questions could be used:

○ What is the history behind this idea/practice/place?
○ What does it tell us about life in Britain today?

This can help students enquire and communicate as well as participate responsibly as they develop understanding of national and international identities.

Key reading:
Arthur, J., Davies, I., Wrenn, A., Haydn, T. and Kerr, D. (2001) *Citizenship through Secondary History*. London: Routledge.

The politics of place is a very important way of understanding contemporary society. Who lives where is for many a very obvious citizenship-type question. One idea for classroom work would be to choose something from the local area and ask students to explore why it has appeared.

Take a map of two contrasting suburbs either real or imagined, close to the school or from another part of the country, depending on the issues you want to raise. Provide, or ask students to research, some background information (examples of estate agents' information about houses in the two areas; crime rate; results achieved by local schools; number of people unemployed, etc.).

Highlight, or ask students to identify, certain features on a map such as hospitals, schools, leisure centres, transport routes and shops. Then ask the pupils to draw up a list of factors that might have led to people living in one or the other of these areas. They will perhaps mention economic factors such as closeness to place of work, house prices; personal factors such as location of family or friends; environmental factors such as desire to be in the countryside or city; or there may be other factors to do with political or cultural issues.

Finally, a discussion could be held about the distribution of scarce goods that is occurring in these different contexts. Another exercise could be based, loosely, on town planning in which students are asked to develop their own ideas about what could and should be provided in a local area. These ideas can be extended to include global and environmental issues.

Key reading:
See Lambert, D. and Machon, P. (2001) *Citizenship through Secondary Geography*. London: Routledge, for some ideas and examples of classroom work. Look also at the websites of the Geographical Association and the Royal Geographical Society.

There are many connections between language and power, stories and culture and communication and social issues. Therefore, there's a very close link to English in the skills element of the citizenship curriculum (e.g. how to express an opinion in writing and verbally).

Ask your students to analyse the ways in which a politician answers questions by watching a brief excerpt from a televised interview. They should focus on:

o body language;
o length of answer;
o number and type of interruptions (by interviewer or interviewee);
o use of factual information;
o use of emotional language;
o explanations of what has been done in the past;
o promises of what will be done in the future;
o personal statements that might be used to gain support;
o negative statements about self or others;
o positive statements about self or others.

Or, devise a brief scenario that leads to the need for a written complaint. Ask students to compose such a letter considering what's put in the first and last sentence and paragraph (these are usually the spaces for summary statements); what sort of evidence is used in the letter; what sort of language (detached, formal or emotional?); and to whom should it be addressed.

Some students could also analyse the differences between submissions that might be made to a broadsheet compared to those to a tabloid newspaper.

Key reading:
Moss, J. (2001) *Citizenship through Secondary English*.
London: Routledge.

The latest science programmes emphasize the value of science for citizens. The Wellcome Institute has funded initiatives in which science and citizenship are explored, and the Association for Science Education has promoted context-based approaches to science and, more specifically, the ways that young people can develop social and political understanding and action.

Many school projects can easily be suggested:

o a joint geography and science exploration of the siting of a nuclear energy station;
o the advantages and disadvantages of renewable energy (there are currently a number of enquiries into wind farms that can provide a lot of classroom material);
o you could set up a science media watch in which stories are identified and assessed for their science content, with assessments being made for what is being claimed (what is said to be true; what is said to be harmful; what is said to require further investigation).

Key reading:
Fullick, P. and Ratcliffe, M. (eds) (1996) *Teaching Ethical Aspects of Science*. Southampton: Bassett Press.
Levinson, R. and Reiss, M. J. (eds) (2003) *Key Issues in Bioethics: a guide for teachers*. London: Routledge Falmer.
Ratcliffe, M. and Grace, M. (2003) *Science Education for Citizenship*. Maidenhead: Open University Press.

There are a number of different approaches that can be used to explore the connection between mathematics and citizenship.

1 Perhaps the most difficult to explore is the notion that mathematics is not objective knowledge but just as culturally determined as other subjects. Academically this is known as ethno-mathematics and explores our reliance on what is essentially an Arabic heritage of mathematical understanding. It can be provocative for students to realize that forms of counting and other basic elements are not somehow 'God-given' but the result of particular forms of understanding gaining preference over others. If citizenship is, at least in part, about understanding power then this sort of awareness about how we come to accept certain ideas is very relevant.

2 The skills of mathematics can be developed in real life situations: you cannot work out income tax, the change that should be received in a shop or fair shares for three people, etc. if you don't have some basic mathematical knowledge and understanding.

3 Also, more direct use of mathematics for citizenship purposes can be explored. For example, when a school has undertaken a mock election the mathematics department can be useful not only in counting the votes but showing the extent of any 'swing', the proportions of people who have voted and what would have happened if a variety of systems had been used (for example, first past the post as opposed to single transferable vote).

If citizenship education is in part concerned with ensuring young people are prepared for life in a democratic, pluralistic and multi-faith society, then religious education (RE) is important for its development.

Here are three classroom ideas.

1 Research about one or more communities could lead to role-plays, for example a wedding. Follow up with group discussions based on key questions like: what according to the different individuals and groups involved is the purpose of marriage? What is the link between theology and social convention (are there any consistencies and inconsistencies)? Who has the power to make decisions at crucial points in the process? Who currently is excluded from wedding ceremonies (this principally applies to the gay community) and is this acceptable? Given the rate of divorce, is marriage now an outdated concept?

2 A visit to a local cemetery can lead to valuable work on identity and power. What symbols are being used on the graves? Does the cemetery reflect the nature of the local population, or does this link with geography not apply? What do the graves tell us about the religious beliefs of that community? And so on.

3 Case studies can be developed to explore the link between citizenship and religious practice, for example, the decision by the French government to ban the wearing of religious symbols in schools. Also the last few decades in Northern Ireland's history supplies rich data for investigation.

RELIGIOUS EDUCATION

STATISTICS

Many of the comments made in Idea 25 also apply here, but some greater specialist knowledge can be expected when students are studying statistics. Some classroom activities are outlined below.

The class could work on averages, modes and medians that follow the health of individual businesses or the whole economy during periods of office of different governments. It would then be interesting to explore the claims made by politicians in relation to their own records and those of their competitors. This information (or some of it) is regularly included in publications such as the *Economist* and in the speeches of politicians.

It would be inappropriate to assume that simple predictions can be made about the behaviour of consumers or voters, but some basic work on probability could be done in relation to voting patterns during the last few decades. It is easy to obtain figures about the extent to which different age groups have voted during the last few general elections. On the basis of these figures, how likely is it that more than 50 per cent of 18–24 year olds will vote in the next general election? How does this compare to the actual result?

A good deal is heard about immigration and asylum seekers. Some rather alarmist headlines from newspapers can set the scene prior to an investigation into the proportion of immigrants in the total English, Welsh, Scottish, Northern Irish and European populations. The proportion of immigrants to countries such as Canada, as well as various low-income countries, will provide plenty of interesting issues to debate.

Using the technique known as Spearman's rank, students can be asked if preferences for different political parties are erratic or consistent when considered over several themes such as health, education and defence.

The processes of physical education (PE) can be enormously relevant to citizenship education. One only has to think of the caricature of the games teacher in the film *Kes* to know how one can easily work against the values of citizenship.

A lot of nonsense is written about the so-called determination of trendy teachers to abandon competition and insist only on collaborative games (one high profile commentator has sneered at the supposed notion that 'all must have prizes'). But cooperation is important. Competition and collaboration are not polar opposites and students can easily be alerted to the sort of teamwork that is required before victory (either in terms of good sporting behaviour, or in the sense of winning against another team). PE teachers have a good deal to teach us in how they decide to organize skill-based sessions. But be careful – just organizing a team game is not necessarily citizenship education.

Health education can be a key feature of citizenship education if it's considered in a societal – rather than merely a personal – context. PE teachers can tell us about the best ways in which a healthy body can be created and preserved. It is only in the examination courses related to PE that the issues associated with individual health and the wider society can be probed (connections with taxation to be paid to the National Health Service, the link between diet, commerce and longevity, etc.).

All teachers can in a positive way encourage some sort of reflection upon these matters.

PHYSICAL EDUCATION

DESIGN AND TECHNOLOGY

Innovative designs are successful only when there's an acceptance of a positive impact on society. The link with citizenship is therefore very clear, as it's a political – as well as a simple design – issue to decide what should be regarded as a positive technological development. The days are long gone of students producing a cake slice for the purpose of filling low-status lesson time and providing parents with a moment of pride. Assessing need, developing an idea into something that could be made, testing and refining a prototype and producing the final version that will be subjected to a rigorous evaluation by users are the normal procedures that drive many lessons.

Many examples could be given of successful work but I'll give only one instance here. A student visited a vet's surgery to investigate the possibilities of creating a new design. A long process eventually resulted in the design and manufacture of a device that would hold open a dog's mouth during surgery. The value of such work was clear for the design and technology teacher. The citizenship element was met by the determination of the students to ask challenging questions about the ethical procedures required, and questions about who set these parameters and whether they could be altered. These ethical procedures included asking questions about the relationship between vet and customer and animal.

I have often been pleasantly surprised at the massive potential for collaboration between citizenship teachers and modern foreign languages (MFL) specialists. Three ideas spring to mind:

o Shared projects between schools to investigate, by email discussion, a controversial issue. For example, how do young Germans think about the contemporary significance of the Holocaust?
o Explore the meaning of extracts from relevant literature. For example, the work of Lorca, Camus, and – perhaps only for the really ambitious even if just using extracts – what are we told about justice, morality and responsibility by Dostoevsky's *Crime and Punishment*?
o During an exchange programme arrange for investigations to take place into local or national issues. For example, an exchange with a school in the Loire Valley could lead to work on the relationship between wine, health and the French economy, or, alternatively, a debate about the siting of nuclear power stations in areas of natural beauty.

MODERN FOREIGN LANGUAGES

Developing students' skills

POLITICAL LITERACY

A politically literate person will know what the main political disputes are about; what beliefs the main contestants have of them; how they are likely to affect him [sic] and he will have a predisposition to try to do something about it in a manner at once effective and respectful of the sincerity of others. Put another way the teaching should help to develop empathy about other political viewpoints and to give people a knowledge of the actual political conflicts of the day; some language or system or concepts with which to express themselves critically about these problems and neither to expect too much or too little from their own action.

(Crick and Porter 1978, p. 33)

Civics (as information about political systems) is important but it should be kept firmly in its place. The politics of everyday life – issues about power in the school, the local community and the world – are very important.

The island game is a well-known way of introducing often very young children to systems of government and key political concepts. It involves asking students to imagine they've been shipwrecked on a desert island and then to consider who they would want to be in charge: the strongest/bravest/most intelligent? And would that person be chosen by all, a few or by some sort of contest?

Difficult notions associated with democracy, oligarchy and dictatorship are explored by the students within a short time.

Ted Huddleston (2004) in an excellent pack of political literacy materials has used a summary of Ibsen's *An Enemy of the People* to ask how politicians should respond to the media when it's been discovered that a problem has developed with a town's water supply. Other examples of political literacy work can be seen elsewhere in this book in, for example, Sections 6 and 10.

Key reading:

Crick, B. and Porter, A. (1978) *Political Education and Political Literacy*. London: Longman.

Huddleston, T. (2004) *Citizens and Society*. London: Hodder and Stoughton.

One example developed from the work of Lawrence Kohlberg is shown below. More can be read about the (rather controversial) levels of thinking that Kohlberg proposed. Ask the students to read the following dilemma and then answer the questions that follow.

A person was near death from a special kind of cancer. There was one drug that doctors thought might save the person. It was a form of radium that a druggist in the same town had recently discovered. The drug was expensive to produce, but the druggist was charging ten times what the drug had cost to make. The sick person's friend, Alex, went to other people to borrow the money, but could only get half of the price. Alex told the druggist that his friend was dying and asked for it to be sold cheaper or allow for payment to be made later. But the druggist said: 'No, I discovered the drug and I'm going to make money from it'. So Alex got desperate and broke into the druggist's store to steal the drug for the sick person.

Would you steal the drug to save your friend's life?

Questions and issues to consider:

o How would you introduce this activity to pupils? Would you explain the purpose of the exercise?
o Would you lead the exercise with the whole class? Would pupils work in small groups? Would pupils need to record decisions in writing (or some combination of these approaches)?
o Do you say that some pupils have reached the right answer? Do you refer to levels of thinking? Do all pupils get to see the levels that you and/or Kohlberg recommend at the end of the exercise?
o Kohlberg suggested that higher-level thinking involved a recognition of key principles to do with justice; lower levels involve a simple recognition of the existence of rules or laws and a desire to avoid punishment. What do you think?

More can be read about Kohlberg's work at: http://faculty. plts.edu/gpence/html/kohlberg.htm.

SOCIAL AND MORAL RESPONSIBILITY

Becoming involved in the community (local, national, global) is an excellent way to help students understand, enquire and act. Ask them to consider the following.

The children of Leafy Lane Primary School (LLPS) are looking forward to going to Good Results Comprehensive School (GRCS). LLPS is in a village or suburb based four miles away from GRCS. There has been a link for the last 30 years between these schools. GRCS is a well-regarded school and has achieved in recent years a great deal both academically and socially. The school is over subscribed and new housing is about to be developed in the area.

The local council feels that GRCS has too many pupils. It also sees that other local schools, especially Town Comprehensive (TC), would benefit from attracting more pupils. TC doesn't achieve results similar to those at GRCS. TC is situated in a fairly pleasant area but with many more social problems than the areas that feed into GRCS. It is suggested that children in the LLPS area should in future feed into TC.

A local action group is started by parents of LLPS. They demand that their link with GRCS is maintained. Teachers at GRCS have mixed views about this. Many believe in the value of comprehensive education and feel that GRCS may be developing into a grammar school with selection by postcode. Some are wary of the motives of the local council, suspecting that financial issues rather than educational priorities are governing decision making. Some are wondering about the impact of changing catchment areas on the nature of the school and the results that can be achieved in the future.

The students and teachers following a citizenship education course at GRCS decide to investigate the issue. Many of the pupils at GRCS attended LLPS some years ago. A campaign group is quickly formed by school students. This group may be assisted by a number of parents. A press release is issued by students. The council is accused of 'social engineering'. Students, acting independently from teachers, organize a campaign of letter writing to local councillors. In those letters less than wholly positive comments are made about the achievements of TC. Several of the meetings of the parents' action group are attended by school students. A local council meeting is disrupted by shouting from students from GRCS. The head of TC complains to the head of GRCS. Two student members of the school council (representatives of Year 7 and Year 11) propose that the council pass a motion to support the actions of those who have written the letters.

Then ask your students: 'How does this specific issue and the more general matter of community involvement relate to citizenship education?' They can then consider the processes they've engaged in and their developing understanding and skills as citizens.

1 What arguments were put forward?
2 What characterizes a good (and not so good) argument?

GROUP DISCUSSIONS

Citizenship is characterized by positive, active and knowledgeable participation. One obvious way to generate this involvement is through discussion. Many interesting and valuable interactions can occur if people are asked to discuss collaboratively a challenging problem.

An example of such a problem, adapted from Plous (1993), is as follows:

> *A man bought a chair for £60 and sold it for £70.*
> *Then he bought it back for £80 and sold it for £90.*
> *How much profit did he make?*

Quite a lot of useful discussion can take place around the ways in which the group operates to come to a decision: does one person dominate; do all voices carry equal weight, etc? The above example has been chosen because it normally leads to a rapid response from an individual. It then requires another individual to intercede with a different answer before discussion leads to a resolution. When another more value-laden scenario is used one can begin to reveal many more issues (and, probably more valuable matters).

Key reading:
Plous, S. (1993) *The psychology of judgement and decision making.* New York: McGraw Hill.

When should people speak and when should they keep quiet? If students have a good idea, when is the best time to introduce it? Should they seize the moment and speak as soon as a relevant thought pops into their head? Should they wait until they've thought things through and risk the meeting moving onto other business?

A different question about when to speak concerns formal inputs into debates. If citizenship is concerned, at least in part, with making one's voice heard then it's very useful to help students develop an ability to contribute to debates. Some would argue that speaking first allows you to set the agenda before people become bored or confused. Others suggest that a decision to speak last means you can use the ideas of the people who have spoken before and you have the opportunity to leave the audience with your ideas ringing in their heads. There is probably no single best way to proceed especially as these matters are so dependent upon particular contexts. However, one review of research suggests:

If you are offered the chance to speak first or last in a public debate, you should speak first if the other side will follow you immediately and there will be a delay in the debate and people's responses to it. For example, if you are debating an issue that will be voted on in a week, then you should choose to speak first. On the other hand, if some time will separate the two communications and if people will be asked to act immediately after the second presentation you should capitalise on the 'regency effect' and choose to go last.

(Plous 1993, p. 44)

Key reading:
Plous, S. (1993) *The psychology of judgement and decision making*. New York: McGraw Hill.

UNDERSTANDING BIAS

If citizenship is about discussion and debate, students will need to be able to show some sophistication in their analysis of one-sided presentations. At times people can be persuaded that something looks better than it really is. Does this mean that when presentations are being made, students should not only to listen to what's being said but also to think about the context and the ways in which it's being presented? Consider the examples below.

○ Contrasting images: a presenter may decide to talk about a bad thing before discussing the policy or idea to be introduced. Occasionally, estate agents are accused of this sort of tactic by showing a very expensive property, or a run down one, before they 'reveal' the house they really want to sell. It is very easy to model this sort of approach by using estate agents' literature on two properties.

○ Making more of your track record than is really justified. If a teacher or student wants to persuade others to agree with something, do they spend a great deal of time not talking about the issue at hand but about successes that occurred elsewhere?

○ Using factual information selectively. When a person wants to present a case that seems 'solid', hard data may be used. But what is being omitted?

○ Using emotional language. What sort of emotional appeals do politicians make?

For an interesting discussion about political communication, including matters not presented here, such as body language and audience response, see Bull, P. (2003) *The microanalysis of political communication: claptrap and ambiguity*. London: Routledge.

Participation is the principal but elusive goal of many who are involved in citizenship education, but what does it mean? It is a challenging area that should explicitly inform all the work that is done in citizenship education.

Levels of participation (taken from Hart 1992) can be seen as follows:

1   Manipulation. Children are engaged or used for the benefit of their own interests, formulated by adults, while the children themselves do not understand the implications.
2   Decoration. Children are called in to embellish adult actions. Adults, do not, however, pretend that all this is in the interest of the children themselves.
3   Tokenism. Children are apparently given a voice, but this is to serve the child-friendly image adults want to create, rather than the interest of the children themselves.
4   Assigned but informed. Adults take the initiative to call in children but inform them on how and why. Only after the children have come to understand the intentions of the project and the point of their involvement do the children decide whether or not to take part.
5   Consulted and informed. Children are intensively consulted on a project designed and run by adults.
6   Adult initiated, shared decisions with children. In the case of projects concerned with community development, initiators such as policy makers, community workers and local residents frequently involve various interest groups and age groups.
7   Child initiated and directed. Children conceive, organize and direct a project themselves without adult interference.
8   Child initiated, shared decisions with adults.

Ask students to review situations with which they are familiar and judge the number in the above list that could be applied. Teachers will know the sort of situations that can realistically be identified for discussion. In some schools it will be possible to discuss the school itself; in others it may be necessary to distance

PARTICIPATION

the discussion somewhat by, for example, talking about the local council, the relationship between voters and the government, the input that is possible in imaginary families, etc.

Key reading:
Hart, R. (1992) *Children's Participation: the theory and practice of involving young citizens in community development and environmental care*. London: Earthscan.

An important part of citizenship education for a
democracy is to develop understanding and skills
associated with a diverse society. This is such an
important matter that it should feature in almost all
sessions. It also needs explicit consideration, and one
example of classroom work is shown below.

Undertake a review of the representation of Islam in
the media (perhaps a good example would be the speech
made by David Bell, chief inspector of Ofsted, about
Islam and citizenship – see www.ofsted.gov.uk/
publications/index.cfm.). Categorize the reports in the
following way:

1   Description: What is the report about? Where has the
    report appeared (name of newspaper, TV station)?
    When was the report made? How high a profile did
    the report have (minutes or column inches and on
    what page or what position in the TV news)?
2   Judgement: Is the report biased, accurate, fair and
    reliable? It will be necessary to help students to find
    supplementary evidence so that they can make this
    judgement.
3   Implications: What will this report lead to? Will
    people respond positively to Islam in light of this
    report or react negatively?
4   Action: What should be done in light of this report?
    Do the students think that some sort of action should
    be taken against those named in the story or should
    action be taken against the media?

UNDERSTANDING DIVERSITY

EFFECTIVE SUPPORT FOR SPECIAL EDUCATIONAL NEEDS STUDENTS

Citizenship explores and promotes inclusion. There is general guidance from government agencies, such as the QCA, and some interesting practical suggestions have been produced that focus directly on citizenship.

A series of very useful ideas about the connection between citizenship education and special educational needs, written by Lee Jerome, has been placed on the citizED website (see www.citized.info). Jerome recommends that attention be paid to differentiation in which resources, classroom layout, language, teaching approaches, etc. are all pitched at a level appropriate to the students in the class.

There are some who regard certain work as being completely unsuitable for some learners but I tend to feel that Jerome Bruner was right when he argued a long time ago that it's possible to focus on valid concepts with all learners and that to avoid doing so would be to practise an unacceptable form of exclusion. What needs to be changed is not the concept that is to be learned but rather the way in which it's explored. This means that the lessons that we would teach with all learners are suitable for those with special educational needs as long as we have paid appropriate attention to language level, the amount of material to be used and the level of independence to be experienced by learners.

Key reading:
Resources on the Institute for Citizenship website:
www.citizen.org.uk/education/senresources.html.
Fergusson, A. and Lawson, H. (2003) *Access to Citizenship: curriculum planning and practical activities for pupils with learning difficulties*. London: David Fulton.

Much of the comment in Idea 39 about students with special educational needs applies to those who are regarded as being gifted and/or talented. It is important to find the right activity for different types of learners rather than imagine that we can somehow have parallel learning.

There is general guidance, and also guidance for individual subjects, given on the QCA website at www.nc.uk.net/gt/index.html. Interestingly, the list of subjects for which there is guidance does not yet include citizenship. However, I think it's possible to consider developing work for citizenship by planning along three dimensions: responsibility (there should be less direction for those who have the potential to chart their own routes); knowledge (expectations about the amount that is known should be much greater); and reflection (there should be a sense in which responses are nuanced rather than superficially generalized, but also that diverse threads of an argument or issue can be pulled together).

EFFECTIVE SUPPORT FOR GIFTED AND/OR TALENTED STUDENTS

Whole-school approaches

CHARITABLE ACTIVITY

It is enormously difficult to discuss charitable activity without giving the misleading impression of suggesting going back to earlier and unhelpful versions of citizenship education in which young people were expected merely to step in where the welfare state was failing. I also do not want to include one charity over another (although one is highlighted below).

Key questions include: Do we have responsibility for others, and if so, who? What are the problems (as well as the benefits) of charitable donations? What links can be made between charitable work and global and environmental issues? How can we support charitable work and at the same time portray the developing world as richly diverse?

In light of the above I would like to give one example of a charity that could be explored. Giving Nation is a project supported by government agencies that provides paper resources and activities for schools. Their website is: www.g-nation.co.uk/teachers/.

They are advertising G-Week. This is a nationwide celebration of giving in schools. It provides an opportunity to recognize pupils' achievements for charity and community.

The titles of their classroom resources are shown below:

o Topic 1: What is charity? Charities and charity – the who and the why.
o Topic 2: Who wants to change the world? Charity as a power for transformation.
o Topic 3: How do charities make a difference? How charities work in practice.
o Topic 4: How do charities gather support? Publicity and promotion: how would you do it?
o Topic 5: People power! Numbers and skills needed to make a change.
o Topic 6: Giving Nation Action Plan – what will you do now that you know how?

In a sense, all those involved in citizenship education are part of an action group. They want to make something happen. However, there's a difference between allowing students to develop knowledge and skills for the purpose of exploring key issues, and promoting a particular outcome that might have political connotations. The latter is normally to be avoided, although there are some who claim that citizenship education can only be meaningful if it emerges from involvement in real political processes.

We also need to be aware that seeming to be inactive – think of Gandhi, and perhaps also knowledgeable voters who show their disapproval of the governing party by not voting – can be as important a feature of citizenship as being active. I think it's important to stress that in educational contexts reflection is a vital part of the process, for example:

○ Why did I take part?
○ Should others have taken part as well?
○ Did my involvement make things better or worse?
○ What evidence am I using as I develop answers to these questions?

Participation itself is ultimately, in school contexts, about what people learn from that participation.

It is possible for schools to establish local branches of organizations such as Amnesty International or Greenpeace. Or you could review several websites with perhaps an invitation to a few speakers that might help clarify issues about participation. What do they find positive or helpful? What really gets in the way of their work?

SCHOOL LINKS/TWINNING

Many organizations are interested in helping schools work together and should be done in the spirit of positive collaboration as an aspect of global citizenship education. The British Council, European Union, Oxfam, Action Aid and many others are available to work with teachers. Government departments may also be helpful. The Department for International Development, for example, shows on its website (www.globaldimension.org.uk) an example of a school for young children that linked with a school in Montserrat.

Good work can be undertaken electronically without ever leaving the home classroom. I think exchange schemes have the power to change lives. I have been involved with schemes that allowed teachers and students to make links with many different countries. There are of course problems that must be overcome to do with resources and ensuring that the requirements of the home institution's programme can be met while individuals are abroad, as well as the many 'everyday' matters to do with personal safety and secure identity.

Issues of national and global citizenship become very apparent when students move from one country to another. A critical but positive approach should be developed so that students do not merely marvel at the 'other'. Queen's University in Canada produces a helpful booklet that helps people prepare for study periods abroad.

Key reading:
A description of one exchange scheme involving student teachers of citizenship can be seen in Davies, I. *et al.* (2003) 'International citizenship education: changing priorities exchanging teachers', in Brown, K. and Brown, M. (eds) *Reflections on citizenship in a multilingual world*. London: CILT.

Peer mentoring is a system where individual students are identified as being able to assist others in the resolution of problems. At times teachers select peer mentors, arguing they need to be sure there's a diverse mix of students. But many feel the selection of the peer mentoring team should be left entirely to the student body itself and decided through the process of an election.

The mentors will need communication and conflict resolution skills and should be genuinely interested in raising the self-esteem of their peers and contributing to the improvement of the school ethos. The mentors will help the student voice to be heard. Training will be required for all those who take on the role.

There are different types of involvement including peer learning, peer mentoring (often for social issues) and conflict resolution. While it may be worthwhile for teachers to take responsibility for the training, this may also be done by existing peers (especially if the scheme has been running for some time) and perhaps through the involvement of an outside agency (see Mediation UK: mediationuk@cix.compulink.co.uk).

Teachers and others need to be alert to the difficult issues that may arise, such as misunderstandings and concern from parents and others about the revelation of what might be regarded as confidential information during peer involvement.

PEER MENTORING

Key reading:
Some useful examples of peer mentoring are given in Clough, N. and Holden, C. (2002) *Education for Citizenship: ideas into action. A practical guide for teachers of pupils aged 7–14.* London: Routledge Falmer.

The combination of all the work suggested in this book is, hopefully, the way to establish an appropriate classroom atmosphere or ethos. The achievement of this elusive goal is probably the acid test of citizenship education. But we should be honest and realistic and accept that, like patriotism, an argument that a school 'delivers' its citizenship education programme solely through ethos is probably the last refuge of a scoundrel. Nevertheless, ethos is a key factor for citizenship education and, moreover, one that can be responsible for helping improve academic results (see Trafford 1993).

It is for each school to decide upon their preferred ethos and work towards it. I do not believe that it's essential for completely democratic procedures to be in place before one can claim that an appropriate ethos has been achieved. The following gives an indication of what, according to one author (Fletcher 1989), is a democratic school:

○ active, critical school council;
○ fully participative staff in which they can shape the agenda;
○ heads that are committed to emphasize principles not details, tirelessly 'explaining' the school and confidence in staff and others;
○ parents that are regarded as partners with rights of open access to the school and elected to key positions;
○ governors that are elected and discuss in a body where no single group holds an effective majority.

Key reading:
Trafford, B. (1993) *Sharing Power in Schools: raising standards.* Ticknall: Education Now.
Fletcher, C. (1989) 'Democratisation on Trial', in Jensen, K. and Walker, S. (eds) *Towards Democratic Schooling: European Experiences.* Milton Keynes: Open University Press.

There *is* such a thing as society but, of course, it's probably better to recognize that within any community (local, national or global) there are different groups and sometimes fairly difficult tensions. It may be unwise to invite someone into the school for a brief question and answer session just in order to pretend that there are good relations with the local community. Better perhaps to set up some sort of discussion or other activity, for example, linked recycling projects or reading schemes for the elderly or very young.

I have seen Question Times work very well in a project managed by the Institute for Citizenship. In these events, local schools were invited to prepare questions for an invited panel that would include young people but also a representative of the police, residents' group, local council and social services. The panel is usually subjected to a pretty intense informed grilling. With careful preparation and follow up these events can be very successful for the students of all the schools invited.

WORKING WITH THE LOCAL COMMUNITY

SCHOOL ASSEMBLIES

These can link with many of the activities outlined in this book. For example, question time events, school council activities, arrangements for mock elections and much else can be focused through assemblies. Of course, other possibilities exist. A series of invited speakers can give a ten-minute talk on a particular theme. A teacher or student can give an account of what could be called 'issue (or thought) for the day' based on a topical news story.

A brief role-play can take place to explore reactions to something in the school or local community that is currently regarded as problematic. For example, it's possible for simple perennial issues, such as which year groups are asked to go into the dining room before others, to be considered from different view points. Or perhaps more challenging, a presentation with discussion around the decision of the local council to change a leisure centre into a hotel and casino.

If genuine participation is not being practised (e.g. if students are merely listening to teachers lecturing them about the need to take part), then citizenship education is perhaps not taking place or not being fully explored.

There are however, some dangers with participation to avoid.

○ First, if we involve students it should be done in a way that doesn't mean they'll be seen merely as 'agents' of the staff.
○ Second, any sort of pupil monitor (and monitoring) system may be seen in a negative light.
○ Third, make sure the students are representative of the wider student body.
○ Fourth, development of the knowledge, skills and dispositions of the students charged with responsibility will need to be addressed.
○ Fifth, the extent of their responsibilities and participation should be made clear from the start.
○ Finally, the processes need to be clarified. Are students expected to consult through assemblies? Staff meetings? Be involved in staff appointments or governors' meetings? If handled well this sort of participation allows students to learn how to make their voice heard and to understand how power is deployed.

SPECIAL RESPONSIBILITIES FOR STUDENTS

Governors are a key part of the school but too often they remain rather shadowy figures who are unknown to the student population. A number of ways can be developed to ensure the governance of the school is clear to the students.

○ A governor could be invited to talk briefly and generally to an assembly about the work of the governing body.

○ An annual or termly meeting could be timetabled between the school council and the governing body.

○ Invitations to events that involve the governors could be routinely extended to members of the school council or other school students.

○ Working groups that are established from the whole governing body could include a school student.

○ A governor could be invited to specific citizenship lessons to discuss issues about how the school is managed.

○ More ambitiously (for those who feel that information about schools should always be kept secret), a form of twinning could occur so that a student visits another school's governing body and then reports back to the home school's governing body on what they are doing.

An alternative way of gaining outside input might be to make links between the students, the governors and the person within the LEA who can describe good practice and suggest issues to consider further. As citizenship is often concerned with exploring power, the opportunities available locally to understand more about and to work with those who are powerful should be explored.

Students are keen to become involved in work that relates to the environment. It is possible to involve them in the consultations established by local councils which undertake ward reviews into how budgets should be allocated. Many councils are happy to allow teachers to use the same questionnaires used in these consultation exercises and accept the responses the students make.

It is possible for students to suggest environmental projects as they respond to the local city council or to propose something within the school itself, perhaps through the school council. It is not uncommon for schools to establish surveys into matters such as water management in the school (with recommendations made and targets set). It might be a good idea to emphasize the key elements of the work through a catchy acronym such as ROAR (research; organize; act; reflect).

These sorts of projects can be very positive if they allow for a review of the activities of those who seem to be powerful, as well as merely becoming part of the decision-making process itself. It would be helpful if the work could form part of an annual cycle with decisions made and targets set in autumn, and achievements (or lack of them) reported on by the end of the academic year.

Try to become involved with larger international organizations, such as the World Wildwife Fund (WWF). Explore the implications of what the students are suggesting and doing. Are they pursuing what is known as an eco-centrist approach or are they more inclined to techno-centrism, that is, can technology help us solve our problems or is it the cause of our difficulties? Are they restricting themselves to promoting something like recycling that might implicitly accept, for example, excessive packaging or are they taking a more wide-ranging environmental approach that could have political aspects?

SETTING UP AN ENVIRONMENTAL CLUB

Running a school council

THE PURPOSE OF A SCHOOL COUNCIL

School councils can teach students a great deal about the democratic process and encourage them to practise the skills of participation.

Schools are not democracies, but it's vital to give the impression that students will be able to achieve something through the council. Lessons could be held within the citizenship programme to inform and discuss with all school students the aims, structures and processes that are relevant to a council. Students will need to be told when and how the elections will be managed, what an agenda looks like, how many meetings will be held each term, and so on. A great starter for the class is to discuss what comes into their minds when they hear the term 'school council'? Divide the class into small groups to discuss how they would ensure their preferred vision of a council could develop. Students could also be asked for their thoughts on the following:

○ The council teaches people how to do things such as planning, persuading others, presenting a case, etc. This is a form of political training or education. What skills will the councillors need?

○ A council is a way of allowing young people freedom and responsibility. The essence of this approach is that it helps people to interact with others. The nature of the interaction is personal. It is not important to think about political skills but rather to consider people's ability to get along with others.

○ A council is there to make real improvements in the school. If it fails to make things happen then it's not worth having.

Key reading:

Baginsky, M. and Hannam, D. (1999) *School Councils: the views of students and teachers.* London: NSPCC.

School Councils UK (2001) *Secondary Pupil Council DIY Resource Pack.* London: School Councils UK.

Training sessions with councillors will help them consider the extent of their responsibilities and the limits of what they could achieve. An example scenario: if councillors come to a meeting wanting to argue for the abolition of the school uniform and staff are not even prepared to begin to consider it.

To what extent will the council agenda follow an issue-based format? Or is there to be a common pattern for each meeting based, for example, around year groups? There should be attention to the development of an agenda that recognizes the following:

O the use of appropriate forms of communication and discussion to allow for a positive result;

O the ordering of items so that what's regarded as the most desirable by councillors is given an appropriate position on the agenda.

Councillors have their own constituencies to whom they must report successfully, or, just like a politician who fails to deliver, they will lose authority and respect and the whole system will fail. Consultation can take place with the wider student body about the issues they want to see raised. Consultation can also occur between councillors and members of staff in order to see what issues might be raised. For example:

O whether money raising activities should take place for particular causes;

O whether a non school uniform day is to be held;

O whether it's possible to purchase additional facilities in the library or elsewhere;

O how to respond to difficult matters such as bullying or vandalism.

HELPING COUNCILLORS FORM
AN AGENDA FOR MEETINGS

In the following exercise, which is a slightly modified form of a game described by Plous (1993), participants could be asked to realize that at times people find it very difficult to stop, go back and accept other views. The councillors need to be reminded that the council is also for students to learn to discuss and discuss to learn.

The game is called 'How much would you pay for £1?' There are five rules:

1. No communication is allowed between the bidders while the auction is underway.
2. Bids can only be made in multiples of 5p.
3. Bids must not exceed £5.
4. The two highest bidders would both have to pay what they bid even though the £1 only goes to the highest bidder.
5. Real money is not to be used.

There are two crucial points in the game: when the two highest bids added together exceed £1 (so, the auctioneer is guaranteed a profit) and when one of the bids reaches £1. In the first case the bidders will suffer a collective loss and it's interesting to see whether they decide to continue or not. In the second case it seems odd for a person to continue to bid over £1 even though only £1 can be 'won'. But, if a person feels that they have just lost 95p because their competitor has bid £1, it can appear to be sensible for them to bid just a little more. They may see themselves in competition not with the auctioneer from whom they can gain £1 but rather with another bidder. It suddenly becomes possible for them to rationalize the need to bid a lot more than £1 in order to win this new competition.

The game can be used as an illustration of the way in which those involved in discussion lose sight of what should really matter.

Key reading:
Plous, S. (1993) *The psychology of judgement and decision making*. New York: McGraw Hill.

Ask students to review the constitution of a neighbouring school or their own school after discussion about the nature and purpose of a council.

The following questions might help councillors to focus on some challenging issues:

○ Do you think that the constitution is sufficiently clear about its purpose?
○ Do you think that the constitution distributes power appropriately between staff and pupils?
○ Do you think that there should be other matters included in the constitution (e.g. activities to be undertaken by the council members and the resources available for that work).

The above questions can also be used to review other matters such as peer mentoring schemes.

Following this exercise, students could be asked to undertake a number of tasks:

○ write their own constitution;
○ compare the constitution with the arrangements that are currently in place within their school;
○ interview two pupils from different year groups and two members of staff (one of whom is a member of the council and one who is not) to ask about the purpose of the council, where the balance of power lies and its effectiveness.

STRUCTURES FOR DEVELOPING A SCHOOL COUNCIL

HELPING COUNCILLORS REPORT BACK

There are many simple ways in which councillors can be guided into reporting back effectively. For example:

o Listening to a TV programme and then reporting back the main features. In this way students can practise the skill of remembering and passing on information and ideas.
o Traditional note taking exercises (for which there are many published guides already available) could help.
o Reading a newspaper report and then passing on the key points in a limited time will concentrate minds.

Some discussion about voice (tone, volume, etc.) and body language would help. Attention needs to be paid to reporting to different audiences. Some obvious differences between a report made to a group of younger students and then to a group of staff would be the language level used and also the focus on certain aspects of the report that are felt to be of particular interest to each group.

The context of a presentation needs to be considered: talking with an individual requires a certain style; reporting to a year group in an assembly demands a very different approach. Also discuss the various ways in which messages can become garbled. Deliberate or accidental bias (by omission or inclusion) or inaccuracies can creep into reports. To emphasize this last point it might help, especially with younger groups, to discuss simple optical illusions. Things do not appear the same to all people and councillors need to be aware of different perceptions as they report back.

Setting up a mock election

There are many purposes to a mock election but some of the most obvious are:

○ to promote understanding of party politics;
○ to develop awareness of contemporary issues;
○ to provide opportunities for the demonstration and development of the skills of debate and public speaking.

You could simply present the positive aspects and goals of a mock election campaign to students, but it may be more helpful to ask students to offer what *they* think are the advantages of a campaign and then to prioritize these objectives. Then undertake some very basic work on elections in a citizenship lesson.

○ How many people voted in the last general/local/European elections?
○ What sort of people voted?
○ Why might there be concerns about people voting?
○ Would it be useful to make voting a legal requirement?
○ Should the age at which people are allowed to vote be reduced to 16?

Detailed but very accessible data that would help give answers to all the above questions is available at a number of websites including www.parliament.uk/commons/lib/research.

The websites of the Electoral Commission (www.electoralcommission.gov.uk/your-vote/yourvotefaqs.cfm), the Hansard Society (www.hansard-society.org.uk) and in particular the 'Y vote' pages at www.mockelections.co.uk are very valuable. The Institute for Citizenship also offers good resources (see Idea 13).

It is possible to devise your own activities but signing up to an established programme has advantages. The materials and activities are, of course, already available and even if they're modified there'll be less work needed than if you started from the very beginning. Also, given the potentially controversial nature of elections, it can be useful to have the security of working in ways suggested by respected organizations such as the Hansard Society.

In the past the Federal Trust (www.fedtrust.co.uk) has produced materials on European elections. Cornell University in the USA produced mock election resources on the 2004 US presidential election. (Interestingly according to research undertaken by the Pew Research Centre (www.people-press.org) prior to polling, the 2004 US presidential election aroused most interest among young voters since the early 1970s.)

ORGANIZATIONS THAT OFFER SUPPORT FOR MOCK ELECTIONS

A three week timetable is great as this is the normal length of time between the announcement of the UK general election and polling day. It's essential to plan ahead so that, in advance of the work to be undertaken, agreement has been reached with key members of staff:

○ to go ahead with the event;
○ for use of specific spaces (e.g. for posters to be displayed or for meetings to be held);
○ the extent of the students' involvement.

The following jobs/issues need to be allocated and worked out at an early stage:

○ briefings to staff;
○ choose individuals to work with specific parties;
○ arrange for ballot papers to be printed (including arrangements over postal votes);
○ arrange for staff to manage hustings, count votes and interpret results;
○ announce the election to students and invite nominations;
○ ensure students are involved with staff in the jobs mentioned above (e.g. counting votes and interpreting results);
○ whether to allow students to use their own party labels or to insist on the use of the largest and mainstream political parties;
○ whether all year groups are to be involved, and so on.

It is possible to use different frameworks but the following is one that I've seen work well.

Students arrive at school and go to an assembly (year assemblies work best if there's constituencies based on age groups or allowed for party machines that include several candidates) in which there's an opportunity for final speeches made by candidates. The students may then go to a brief session with their tutor in which ballot papers are distributed and a ballot box is available. This approach guarantees a very high turnout. But it's also possible for ballot boxes to be set up in different locations around the school during morning break and lunchtime. If this latter approach is followed, care would need to be exercised to ensure specific groups were directed to particular polling stations and there were identification checks.

The end of lunchtime should be the latest time allowed for voting to occur, thus the early part of the afternoon is made available for counting of the ballots. The results can then be announced using the system agreed in advance (probably first past the post).

During the next few days a series of interviews can be held with candidates during assemblies or published on the school intranet. Analyses of the results can be undertaken using different systems (e.g. proportional representation) and issues raised about the level of involvement of different groups.

IDEA

60

EVALUATING THE EVENT

There are three key ways in which the event can be analysed.

1   Rather intangible factors should be explored. What was the atmosphere like during the election? Was there a positive sense of involvement, with teachers and students engaged in lively but constructive democratic debate?

2   Simple counting should be undertaken in order to establish the level of involvement. How many posters were displayed? How many people attended hustings? How many and what types of students voted?

3   Educational issues should be probed. What sort of knowledge and skills were revealed? Were speeches of a high quality? Were questions asked that were focused and based on good understanding? Did the posters reflect key issues with appropriate language being used? In this context you're more of an assessor using skills used by English teachers (language), history teachers (political concepts), mathematics teachers (understanding of economic indicators) and science teachers (appreciation of the significance of environmental matters, etc.).

The above three considerations should be analysed by a team of students and teachers. They could take the role of election observers (as occurs in major national elections around the world). It would be interesting to involve others in this process, including governors or, more ambitiously, people from political parties or community groups.

Citizenship lessons

IDEA
61

There used to be a children's TV series in which at moments of crisis someone in a rather frantic manner would exclaim 'anything can happen in the next half hour!' You can use this 'hook' to generate some interest in contemporary news stories and make the very important point that we are always unsure how things will develop.

Choose a recent newspaper story that dealt with a crisis. Describe very briefly the background to the story and then present the class with three alternative outcomes. Two of these should be straightforward and one should allow for a slightly fuller and perhaps more subtle response.

For example, if a politician had been accused of negligence or abuse of office, a story might appear suggesting that he or she should be sacked. Following a brief summary of the key issues in the story the class could be given the following outcomes:

o yes, he or she will be sacked (or made to resign);
o he or she will continue in the job;
o something else . . . please explain.

Keep a record of the final outcome put forward and tell the class as soon as possible what actually happened (try to pick issues that will be resolved quickly).

Some students may complain that they cannot be involved, as their views would never be taken into account while decisions were made. So remind them that public opinion does matter and that we all play a part (however small).

This exercise could lead to a discussion about the nature of our formal democratic system that is largely based on representative rather than participatory processes.

This is a version of Pictionary and students will respond easily and positively to the exercise. Divide the class into two teams.

Each side is asked in turn to draw something that illustrates a person or story from public life or a feature of our democracy. The list of people, or topics to be guessed, by the teams is developed by you beforehand and each one passed to the student who will draw. The other members of the team on the same side as the person drawing are asked to guess what is being referred to. If they guess correctly they're awarded two points. If they fail to guess then the other team have a chance to gain one point.

The first team to receive at least five points is the winner. You can provide a little explanation for each of the drawings once the points have been awarded. The value of this for citizenship depends on the items chosen to be drawn and the quality of the brief explanations given by the students and/or you. The items could be selected in order to provide brief explanations about:

o formal politics (Houses of Parliament, the Queen, European Union flag, symbol of the United Nations);
o contemporary stories (price of oil goes up/down, war, pensions crisis, changes in the health service);
o individuals (scope for all those budding cartoonists who can caricature or accurately represent leading figures).

ODD ONE OUT!

Odd one out exercises are now very common in many classrooms. Provide a list of four words and ask students to choose the odd one out and then to give their reasons for their decision. Some examples of lists are given below (of course, in some cases the names would have to be changed to ensure the activity was up to date and that students would know something about the items).

○ Tony Blair; Gordon Brown; the Queen; Jack Straw (odd one out is the Queen as all others are Labour party politicians).

○ Shopping; voting; playing; travelling (voting is the odd one out as the other activities can be done by people younger than 18).

○ Local council; European Parliament; House of Commons; Greenpeace (Greenpeace is the odd one out as it is a pressure group).

This exercise could be expanded into a full lesson if a long list of items was given with students asked to group them. There will in most cases be a right answer but often it'll be possible to have a range of appropriate responses. The key will be to ensure that the exercise is used as a stimulating platform for explanation and further discussion.

Introduce the class to an issue, trend or story. The material could be drawn from any aspect of the citizenship syllabus.

For example:

○ the number of people who voted in the last election;
○ the price of houses;
○ the rate of inflation;
○ the prospects for war in a particular part of the world.

Distribute (or show on an OHP or the board) a set of faces showing different expressions (happy, sad, confused, frightened). Ask the students to make clear their feelings about a particular issue by selecting one of the faces. They can select a face by drawing it in their exercise book or by a show of hands as the teacher points to each picture that has been displayed on the board. Then ask why they feel that way and what (if anything) they can and will do about it.

With some classes it will be enough to show three fairly obvious emotions by using simple drawings of faces (happy, sad, angry) but of course depending on the ability of the class and your skills as an artist the sky is the limit!

HOW DO YOU FEEL ABOUT THAT?

IDEA

65

SIZZLING SOUND BITE SLOGANS

A great deal of work can be done on the ways in which politicians use language.

Students might enjoy the possibilities of exploring a few of the well-known sayings of politicians. They could read the following and then be asked to choose their favourite and explain why they find it attractive (or explain why they feel it would not work):

Ask not what your country can do for you but what you can do for your country (J.F. Kennedy)

Tough on crime and tough on the causes of crime (Tony Blair)

Where there is discord may we bring harmony.
Where there is error may we bring truth.
Where there is doubt may we bring faith.
Where there is despair, may we bring hope (Margaret Thatcher after St Francis of Assisi)

Never in the field of human conflict has so much been owed by so many to so few (Winston Churchill)

I may have the body of a weak and feeble woman but I have the heart and stomach of a king (Elizabeth I)

Students may be interested to see how often a word or phrase is used three times: look at the above example in the quotation by Churchill when 'so' is used three times or think about Blair's 'education, education, education'. Look also for sharp contrasts (the quotation from Thatcher is a whole series of contrasting opposites). A development of the use of contrast can be seen in what I tend to think of as 'turning the phrase': the examples from Kennedy and Blair shown above illustrate the way a reordering of the sentence gives the listener a puzzle to work out as well as a contrast to learn.

There is a whole series of lessons that could be based around citizenship and literacy or citizenship and media studies.

Key reading:

Beard, A. (2000) *The Language of Politics*. London: Routledge.

The highlighting of key objectives throughout the lesson is now an established part of a teacher's repertoire and the use of Post-it notes to emphasize specific points is widespread.

For a citizenship lesson you may have asked the students to think about freedoms in society today and have involved the class in a series of activities which allowed them to consider 'freedom from' and 'freedom to'. Students could have examined groups or individuals in society who want different things. One group could want the freedom to do certain things but another group could object by claiming they want the freedom from being dominated by their opponents.

There are many simple or complex ideas that can emerge from such a lesson (or series of lessons). At the end of a lesson you might want to know more about the reaction of the class and could simply ask them to put their Post-it notes on a screen. They could ask questions, refer to additional contexts that had not been mentioned in the lesson or give their own views about which of the opposing groups they feel to be in the right.

This could provide useful material for an end of lesson discussion or show you what needs to be clarified. A more structured approach would be for you to ask 'what have you learned this lesson?' and insist that all students reply (giving a named slip of paper to you as they leave the room would allow for a reasonably high chance of a considered response). Or, you could remind students of the learning objectives for the lesson and ask for students to give a mark out of ten to show how confident they now feel about understanding that objective.

One way to generate students' understanding of opinion poll data is to allow them to devise a questionnaire of their own. As a fully fledged exercise this could take a considerable amount of time as easily six or seven lessons could be covered by discussing the use of opinion polls, the ways in which questions can be devised and how the results can be analysed.

I think an excellent lesson can be devised solely around the question of what does it mean if I've just told an opinion pollster 'I don't know?' Very good ideas can be developed about 'don't know' meaning a lack of knowledge, a refusal to cooperate or a high level of awareness that has led to difficulty in making a decision about a controversial issue. It is possible to give some very quick activities about questions and how they can be used. One brief activity is to provide a list of flawed questions and then ask students to spot the errors. An example is shown in the box opposite.

Of course, all the questions shown opposite are hopeless. For a start, the first 200 people met in a shopping centre on a Friday morning would not give a representative group. It would be unwise to insist that all questions must be answered (although one can do one's best to achieve a full response). The first question gives overlapping age boundaries and excludes those who are younger than 15 or older than 75 (it's acceptable to deliberately exclude certain people for specific reasons but there is no justification for this given here). The second question asks for more than one response but only allows one simple answer. The third question is a leading question.

The fourth question is very difficult to answer (and the answers would be very difficult to interpret) as it is given in the form of a negative question. People in some parts of the UK use the negative interrogative frequently in their speech and so care would be needed if the questionnaire is to be read to respondents (students will not always read what is on the page). The last question is full of jargon that will simply confuse respondents.

Many other types of weak question could be developed for students to spot examples of bad practice.

How popular is the prime minister?

The first 200 people met in the central shopping centre on Friday morning will be asked. All those people will answer all the questions shown below.

1 How old are you? Circle one of the categories shown below:

   15–25   25–35   35–55   55–75

2 Do you think the prime minister is doing a better job than the previous prime minister, or do you think he could do a bit better? Circle one of the categories shown below:

   Yes   No   Don't know

3 The prime minister is clearly an intelligent person and most are happy with his performance. Do you agree? Circle one of the categories shown below:

   Yes   No   Don't know

4 Do you not think that the prime minister should spend a little more money on hospitals?

   Yes   No   Don't know

5 Given that the money supply in the UK is subject to a range of factors associated with exogenous growth, how do you think the prime minister should deal with inflation?

EVERY PICTURE TELLS A STORY

Cartoons are full of symbols and the best ones make people laugh, tell people about an issue and make them think more deeply about the underlying political and economic factors in society. But cartoons can be difficult for young people to understand, especially if they're not familiar with contemporary news stories.

You can use pictures in a variety of easier ways. For example, show students a photo from a newspaper. Small groups come to the front of the class, memorize the key features and return to their desks. Give them 30 seconds to write down the main features of the picture and then discuss what they've written (simple description) and what the picture shows (an opportunity for a more analytical response).

Alternatively, each student could be given a photocopy of a picture from a newspaper and asked to label the key features. At times this sort of approach can be used simply to get across the story itself but it can also be used to show how a picture has been taken in a certain way to contribute to a particular version of events. Does a picture of a politician crying arouse our sympathy? Does a picture of a demonstration 'prove' that some people are guilty of violence?

Another approach is to give small groups of students different pictures. A theme could be chosen to illustrate an idea/issue. For example:

o Is the environment in danger?
o Was 2005 a good year?
o Is the economy in good shape?
o Are all countries in Africa poverty stricken?

Each group describes their picture and by doing so makes clear what story is being told. One member of each group is then sent to the other groups to find out what other stories are being told by the pictures. One member of each group remains at 'home' to show the picture to the 'visitors'. The group members return to base and they decide on a final version. The different outcomes are discussed by the whole class.

The local council has decided that the local leisure centre and theatre will be developed. The swimming pool is expensive to maintain and not very well used. There are two other theatres in the small town and there have been increasing problems with attracting famous stars who can pull in the crowds. Large amounts of council tax are being spent on maintaining what seems to be no longer needed.

A successful company, Lively Leisure Ltd. (LLL) wants to build a casino and luxury hotel on the site. Immediately, local residents complain. They like the idea of a leisure centre. It is good for people's health and they say the alternative will lead only to large profits for the company, heavy drinking and noise, especially at the weekends.

Ask the students to form different groups comprising councillors, residents, representatives of LLL and observers in order to prepare for a debate. Councillors, residents and the people from LLL each (in groups) prepare a statement. The statements from each of the groups will make clear what they want to happen and why.

While these statements are being prepared tell the observers that they should focus on the debate and look for two things: what is being said and how effectively the points are being made. Discuss with the observers how to listen carefully and what sort of things to make a note of. The students form small groups of four in which there is one representative from the council, LLL and local residents. Each person in this group of four has one minute to speak. When a statement has been made there's an opportunity for the group to ask questions.

When all statements have been made, there's an opportunity for a discussion within the small group. Throughout, the observer in each group makes notes on what is happening. Without using names the observers feedback to the whole class to let others know what points were made and how well they were made. As the formal statements from the councillors, residents and representatives of LLL are the same in each small group, the observers are not expected to report back on the content of that statement, although that might be discussed once led by you. At the end of the lesson you could draw the threads together about the ways to debate effectively.

WHAT SHOULD WE DO?

Getting students involved in displays is always fun. This could be as simple as displaying their work (posters, or video presentations on special occasions) or asking them to respond to issues in simple ways by having 'true' and 'false' cards which could be raised at specific points in the lesson to show what they think.

Students could be issued with artefacts that relate to a citizenship issue. For a lesson on the environment the following could be used:

○ packaging;
○ a leaflet from a pressure group;
○ a photo of a factory polluting the atmosphere;
○ a supermarket containing goods brought from overseas countries;
○ a car;
○ people going on holiday by aeroplane.

Organize a 'display exchange' in which the students tell each other what they have. A record is made of what is being shown and then you can discuss what the class have found out.

A slightly different approach is to ask students to find something being held by another student that complements their artefact and be ready to explain why they have chosen that link. Another way of thinking about display could include the well-known technique of hot seating. In this activity one student is asked (after everyone has had an opportunity to prepare) to play a certain role. The US president, for example, could be put on the spot by students asking about decisions that led to a particular outcome. But the roles could be much more down to earth and, with care, include local illustrations.

Assessing students

INTRODUCTION TO ASSESSMENT

Assessment is perhaps one of the most challenging issues for those who are concerned with citizenship education. Some have argued that citizenship education is not something that can be assessed. It is hard to know whether to emphasize knowledge, skills or attitudes and what sort of blend of these areas is possible.

There are many general resources. For example, students' work with commentaries can be seen at www.ncaction.org.uk. Perhaps the most influential publication in recent years has been Black *et al.* (2003).

There are various pieces designed specifically for citizenship on the www.citized.info website. For example Ruth Deakin Crick's 'Citizenship, Life Long Learning and Assessment', Peter Brett's 'GCSE Cit. Short Courses: A briefing paper and progress report' and Lee Jerome's 'Planning Assessment for Citizenship Education'. And on the www.teachingcitizenship.org.uk website there's a useful section on assessment from the Association for Citizenship Teaching.

It is quite properly part of our broad roles as teachers to concern ourselves with questions about the extent to which young people are becoming citizens. But I think we need to focus principally on how much students are *learning* about citizenship and how well they're able to show the skills required to get things done, both alone and in working effectively and responsibly with others.

Key reading:
Black, P. *et al.* (2003) *Assessment for Learning: putting it into practice.* Maidenhead: Open University Press.

Of course many will not be comfortable with the idea of using levels, arguing that citizenship does not lend itself to this sort of approach. However, levels can be used for many different purposes and I am not sure that applying them only for the purposes of grading would help. We need to be careful that citizenship education is not reduced to a series of simple tests. Rather, it might be useful to be clear to oneself and one's students about what is to be regarded as an initial characterization of good practice.

This doesn't mean that in the light of experience these considerations cannot be altered. Perhaps students will come up with other and better responses than you'd imagined. It may also be the case that the level of generality suggested in Ideas 73 and 74 are not appropriate for specific cases. There are many other issues to be considered and I have done so in some detail in various other publications. That said, if a student were to be assessed in terms of their capacity to explain citizenship issues, the following in Ideas 73 and 74 might be helpful.

WHAT SORT OF LEVELS CAN BE USED TO UNDERSTAND STUDENTS' RESPONSES?

Further reading:
Davies, I. and Thorpe, T. (2003) 'Thinking and Acting as Citizens', in Roland-Levy, C. and Ross, A. (eds) *Political learning and citizenship in Europe*. Stoke: Trentham.

What would a general framework look like for thinking about students' ability to explain citizenship issues? I suggest the following as a starting point for further discussion:

○ Students are confused by a series of events. They cannot understand why things took place as they did and are unable to make progress. The event just doesn't make sense.

○ Students explain matters in terms of people being right or wrong. Or at times the actors are seen as being simply unintelligent or intelligent. Often those who lose are seen as being wrong and unskilled. Pupils may at this level make simple and at times inappropriate connections. One factor (or a list of separate factors) will explain what happened. There is a description of, for example, a legal process rather than analysis. Things happen because people intend them to happen. There is no real attempt to show how factors and individuals interact.

○ Pupils make deliberate efforts to consider both a range of factors and the way in which they interlock. They consider causation and motivation. They look for the relationship between intention and outcome. They view a range of perspectives. They see that narrative order is important is explaining an event. They consider the nature of the relationship between intention and outcome. They are able to comment upon the meaning of relevant value statements.

It's possible to use the above to highlight a rather traditional and perhaps quite narrow focus on assessment of subject knowledge for citizenship. However, it could be used rather more dynamically by looking for the extent to which students demonstrate their capacity to understand explanations and to offer their own explanations. As such this would mean that knowledge and skills (cognitive and active) are being considered.

We should not be too wary of assessing or evaluating students' involvement in citizenship issues. There is a wealth of experience that can be drawn from contexts such as drama education and a rich variety of vocational education. That said, there is currently a hopeful but very challenging sense in which we are dealing with new ground. As a very tentative beginning I would like to suggest that the following might not be seen as simple levels but rather as areas that might indicate ways to explore matters further.

○ Active thinking/Physical activity: Have the students achieved a critical engagement that necessarily involves practically and academically doing something?
○ Individually generated activity/Working with, or in relation to, others: Can students show individual initiative? Can they work with others?
○ Participation in school/Participation in other contexts: Have the school students got opportunities to take part in a variety of contexts?
○ Participating/Engaging: Are students just taking part or are they really engaged?

We can use a variety of data in considering whether students are achieving success. There will be certain obvious signs of involvement (they perhaps participate in the school council, or we can note the number of contributions they make to discussions, for example) and there will also be ways in which we could use evaluation rather than assessment data (i.e. we can ask them if they felt engaged or were just taking part in the way that they had been directed).

ASSESSING PRACTICAL ENGAGEMENT

REPORTING ON WORK DONE IN CITIZENSHIP

Reporting in an old fashioned sense of writing only a summative account of a student's work would not be appropriate for citizenship education. Rather, as well as allowing for the detailed guidance that only the expert teacher can provide, there should be a genuine attempt to recognize the processes implied by the climate that is suitable for citizenship education. I suggest that this means insistence on the good practice already adopted by other subjects.

First, there should be clarity about what is being assessed. Students should understand the nature of the task, its purpose and the possibilities for initiative on their part to transform it, but also the need for them to be clear about the meaning of the numbering or grading system (should one be used). Second, the report should make clear the nature of what sort of action could or should be taken by a student who wishes to improve in particular areas. In this sense all reports are formative.

Third, there should be, through a variety of processes, involvement by the student in the generation of a judgement. At times this will mean the completion by a student of a stand-alone self-assessment tool that has only informal status. Or there may be room for decisions to be negotiated between teacher and student. It may be possible for the students to write their own self-assessments (although of course this would need to be discussed with a teacher).

Government departments, offices and agencies

DEPARTMENT FOR EDUCATION AND SKILLS

The Department for Education and Skills (DfES) has a citizenship team currently headed by Jan Newton OBE (formerly chief executive of the Citizenship Foundation). The DfES shows on its website a range of resources and information about developments that are of vital interest for teachers. One of those resources will be briefly described, but the whole website is worth a visit (see www.dfes.gov.uk/citizenship/).

The 'school self-evaluation tool' was produced in 2004. Building on research being undertaken by the National Foundation for Educational Research and others it suggests that schools are at different stages of development in relation to citizenship education. Some are at an early stage ('focusing') while others are either 'developing', 'established' or 'advanced'. Descriptions of these different levels are given in relation to leadership, resources and their management, teaching and learning, staff development, monitoring and evaluation and parental/community involvement. This tool can be used by schools to reflect on which level they are, and how they might develop even further.

Teachers will not want to accept all the advice but with a positive and critical perspective this tool will prove to be a useful addition to the school's armoury.

Also on the website listed above, there is a link to a useful citizenship CPD handbook called 'Making Sense of Citizenship'.

The standards outlined in 'Qualifying to Teach' by the Teacher Training Agency (TTA) should be essential reading for all teachers. It provides an indication of what is officially regarded as necessary work for beginning teachers and by implication suggests what needs to be done by more experienced teachers.

The TTA funds the citizED project (www.citized.info). That project is centrally concerned with citizenship education and teacher education. It is divided into four areas of activity: primary; secondary; post-16 and cross-curricular. There are many conferences, workshops and resources being produced and it's possible to gain many practical examples of classroom work by exploring their website. There are induction packs for tutors new to teacher education and there's an academic journal (*International Journal of Citizenship and Teacher Education*) available electronically.

TRAINING AND DEVELOPMENT AGENCY FOR SCHOOLS

OFSTED

The Office for Standards in Education has not always been entirely free from controversy. Hailed by some as the body responsible for preserving and developing high standards, it also attracts fierce criticism. It cannot be ignored and its website contains reports on each school in England and Wales as well as LEAs and providers of teacher education. Inspection reports are now only just beginning to report on citizenship education so it is too early to make any firm statements.

The handbook of guidance for inspections is, however, something that should be reviewed by teachers and details are given on the Ofsted website about 'how we inspect'. Teachers should consider their own results in relation to their own targets (generally and for individuals) but also how this compares across subjects and other schools.

The Qualifications and Curriculum Authority (QCA) maintains and develops the National Curriculum and associated assessments, tests and examinations; and accredits and monitors qualifications in colleges and at work. Its website (www.qca.org.uk) provides detailed material including:

o assessment;
o schemes of work;
o a glossary;
o research;
o a range of what it classes useful documents;
o the Crick Report;
o general information about social science and citizenship.

It released in 2004 some information about post-16 citizenship that is interesting and valuable. Again, while teachers will not want to slavishly follow the schemes of work and other exemplar material, an opportunity would be lost if this were to be completely ignored.

QUALIFICATIONS AND
CURRICULUM AUTHORITY

NO. 10 DOWNING STREET

Not everyone will want to spend huge amounts of time teaching about the formal institutional and constitutional side of politics, but at least some exploration of these matters would be useful. The Number 10 website (www. number-10.gov.uk/output/Page1.asp) offers an easy way for school students to get to know a little about the prime minister and the office. I would not advise too much effort to be devoted to studying the nice photographs in the virtual tour of the house, nor to linger too long on the rather idyllic, hectic 'day in the life of the prime minister' (another photo tour). But the website is attractive, user friendly, up to date with the latest political announcements and offers a facility to email the prime minister.

A simple and straightforward exercise would be for the class to review a set of newspapers for one day, choose an issue that seems to them important and then to express their views by email to the prime minister. The email could be written by an individual following some sort of competition (decided by a vote taken by the class?) or perhaps it's better for a composite message to be generated including the points raised during class discussion.

The UK Parliament is a rich source of material that can be used to develop citizenship education. There is a parliamentary education unit that produces resources for school students and teachers (see www.parliament.uk/directories/educationunit.cfm).

As well as encouraging students to learn about the procedures of parliament (how a bill becomes law, what an MP does and what the difference is between the front- and backbenches), it is also useful to think about the wider picture, such as:

○ individuals (perhaps a case study on a local MP);
○ issues (what sort of security arrangements in light of protests by members of the hunting communities and fathers4justice is appropriate?);
○ key concepts (who really has power within the House of Commons – are the debates necessary and effective?).

Many teachers have established mock parliamentary debates with roles for different political parties and then revealed what actually happened by showing pages from the Hansard record. A visit to the Houses of Parliament (perhaps this is possible only for London based schools?) can be valuable especially if arrangements can be made to be met by your MP and for the students to see something happening in the chamber. If you were to make such a visit it would also be good to include another group of people who are involved in the democratic process (perhaps a pressure group?).

HOME OFFICE

Below is a brief outline of the work of the Home Office which has been summarized from their website.

The Home Office aims:

1 To work with individuals and communities to build a safe, just and tolerant society enhancing opportunities for all and in which rights and responsibilities go hand in hand, and the protection and security of the public are maintained and enhanced.

2 To support and mobilize communities so that, through active citizenship, they are able to shape policy and improvement for their locality, overcome nuisance, anti-social behaviour, maintain and enhance social cohesion and enjoy their homes and public spaces peacefully.

3 To deliver the Department's policies and responsibilities fairly, effectively and efficiently through the most up to date project and day-to-day management, the best use of resources and the development of partnership working.

In its concerns with asylum seekers, a key feature of citizenship (formal legal status) can be examined. Examine specific cases of individuals who have not been granted asylum status (do the students think justice was achieved?) as well as analysing the figures for those entering the country (see www.homeoffice.gov.uk/rds/index.htm) and contrasting them with some of the rather alarmist stories appearing in the media.

The booklet distributed in 2004 to every home in the UK about how to prepare against terrorist attack can spark many lively debates among students. As I was writing this a series of TV programmes were being broadcast in which a team of people faced imaginary emergency situations. This sort of format could be easily reproduced for work in the classroom, with you highlighting fundamental matters such as potential conflicts between liberty and justice.

You might also be interested in the work of the civil renewal unit that is based within the Home Office, as it's centrally concerned with issues of participation (www.homeoffice.gov.uk/comrace/active/civil/index.html).

The purpose of the Foreign and Commonwealth Office (FCO) is to work for UK interests in a safe, just and prosperous world. We do this with some 16,000 staff, based in the UK and our overseas network of over 200 diplomatic offices.

(www.fco.gov.uk/)

FOREIGN OFFICE

An endless range of teaching issues arise from the work of the Foreign Office. At the time of writing (September 2004) Bill Rammell was visiting North Korea. It would be interesting to set up a project around North Korea. Where is it? Who is the political leader? What have Western leaders said about North Korea? Is it really a threat to peace and security? And then more particularly, was it right for a government minister to visit the country? If so, what are the options that are open to the minister and what should he do and not do? Links could be made in these discussions with ideas of global citizenship.

Other obvious issues could emerge from our relationships with the USA, the situation in Iraq, the new constitution for Europe, and so on. Each area could lead to a greater understanding of global issues and the nature of global citizenship.

DEPARTMENT FOR INTERNATIONAL DEVELOPMENT

The Department for International Development (DFID) (www.dfid.gov.uk) is the UK government department responsible for promoting sustainable development and reducing poverty. The central focus of the government's policy, based on the 1997 and 2000 White Papers on International Development, is a commitment to the internationally agreed Millennium Development Goals to be achieved by 2015. These seek to:

o eradicate extreme poverty and hunger;
o achieve universal primary education;
o promote gender equality and empower women;
o reduce child mortality;
o improve maternal health;
o combat HIV and AIDS, malaria and other diseases;
o ensure environmental sustainability;
o develop a global partnership for development.

DFID is very interested in promoting education that will help achieve the goals stated above. As such it shows on its website a global dimension project (www.global dimension.org.uk).

There are also a wide range of excellent curriculum resources (normally not available without purchase) and examples of case studies of work done by many schools.

Her Majesty's (HM) Treasury is responsible
for formulating and putting into effect the UK
government's financial and economic policy. It aims
to raise sustainable economic growth, improve the
prosperity of the nation and create economic and
employment opportunities for all. The Treasury works
to achieve economic stability, low inflation, sound public
finances, efficient public services and a more productive
economy (www.hm-treasury.gov.uk/).

The Treasury wants to promote awareness of its work
and so has sponsored a project called Red Box (see www.
redbox.gov.uk/). The website says:

*Red Box invites visitors to take on management of
The Square. Through playing games and answering
questions students must raise enough money to
maintain, or preferably improve, the services offered
in The Square. Students control their own budget and
thus gain experience of how decisions about tax and
public spending are made.*

*There are two different versions of the website, one
suitable for 7–11 year olds and one for 11–16 year
olds. Both can be used as stand alone ICT resources
or in conjunction with the material provided for each
age group.*

Examination syllabuses

A specification must give opportunities to:

o develop and apply knowledge and understanding about becoming informed citizens through and alongside the development of skills of enquiry, communication, participation and responsible action;

o explore local, national and international issues, problems and events of current interest;

o critically evaluate their participation within school and/or community activities.

A specification entitled Citizenship Studies must make clear the content on which assessment will be based and be consistent with the knowledge, skills and understanding required in the National Curriculum programme of study at KS4 for citizenship for England, and/or the Personal and Social Education Framework for Wales and/or the Northern Ireland curriculum. Specifications for use in Wales should focus on Wales and the curriculum Cymreig. The Edexcel course covers: human rights; power; politics and the media; and the global village. The OCR course covers various issues including rules and laws, community issues, family and school, government and global citizenship.

GCSE specifications in citizenship studies should provide opportunities for developing and generating evidence for assessing the key skills listed below.

o application of number;
o communication;
o information technology;
o improving own learning and performance;
o problem solving;
o working with others.

For further details here and in Idea 87, please see information provided by the Qualifications and Curriculum Authority at:
www.qua.org.uk/2974_2326.html.

The examination boards recommend specific texts. For example:

- o Edexcel has endorsed: Culshaw, J., Wales, J., Clarke, P., Reaich, N. (2002) *Citizenship Today*. London: Collins.
- o OCR has endorsed: Thorpe, T. and Marsh, D. (2002) *Citizenship Studies*. London: Hodder and Stoughton.
- o AQA has endorsed: Mitchell, M., Jones, D. and Worden, D. (2002) *Citizenship Studies*. London: Hodder and Stoughton.

Candidates must be able to:

- o Demonstrate their knowledge and understanding of events of current interest; roles, rights and responsibilities; communities and identities; democracy and government; and relate them appropriately to individual, local, national and global contexts.
- o Obtain, explain and interpret different kinds of information, including from the media, in order to discuss, form and express an opinion formally, and in writing, and demonstrate their ability to analyse and present evidence on a variety of issues, problems and events.
- o Plan and evaluate the citizenship activities in which they have participated and demonstrate an understanding of their own contribution to them as well as recognizing the views, experiences and contributions of others.

The assessment objectives listed above must be (broadly) equally weighted.

Each scheme of assessment must include a terminal, externally assessed component weighted at 60 per cent and an internally assessed component weighted at 40 per cent. Both components must address all of the assessment objectives. All assessment components must be targeted at the full range of GCSE grades.

The three different examination boards can be contacted at:

- o AQA: www.aqa.org.uk.
- o OCR: www.ocr.org.uk.
- o Edexcel: www.edexcel.org.uk.

The content and focus of projects can vary from those that investigate transport issues using the perspectives of local residents, to international enquiries gathering data from school students in other parts of the country or world, to practical engagement that aims to achieve a specific outcome.

Encourage students to work in four key stages:

1 Getting started. Initial thoughts are generated and discussed in which the students ask three questions: Who should I work with? What topic should I work on? What is the type of project to be established (research and/or practical initiative)?

2 A planning phase. Students, either individually or in groups, develop a clear timetable in relation to jobs and, importantly, a set of contingency plans for each stage. Five questions need to be addressed: What role must each person in the team play? What must each person have achieved by specific dates? What resources are needed? Whose permission should be asked? What do we do if things go wrong? Ethical issues should be explicitly considered at this point (e.g. is it right to ask these questions and should the students promise respondents anonymity?). It is also important to consider at this stage practical safety issues if there is to be contact between the students and others.

3 Carrying out the project. If the planning phase has taken place carefully and thoroughly then (fingers crossed) the project itself should run fairly smoothly.

4 Evaluating the project. Emphasize that evaluation should not be undertaken as a last minute activity but should be built in from the very beginning. Students need to ask: What is the key question that I'm addressing? What sort of evidence do I intend to gather? How will I analyse that evidence (e.g. statistical analysis of questionnaire responses or a review of interview data)? What sections do I expect my report to have (and, later in the exercise, what argument am I making)?

Developing good presentation skills is a key element of citizenship education. The presentation of written work should, of course, follow the normal conventions associated with good standards of literacy, but students can also be guided in ways that will allow for a very professional written presentation. The following is a guide to what should be written.

○ Introduction: what question has been pursued; what argument is made in this piece of work; and what are the main subtitles that are used in the piece of writing?
○ Context: what are the big ideas and issues that have led to the development of this piece of work?
○ Methods: what has been done in order to gather data; who formed the sample; what sort of data was used (interviews/questionnaires/news reports, etc); what safeguards were put in place (was data only collected from certain people at specific times of the day and has all data been treated anonymously?)?
○ Issues: what are the key arguments that are being made? Normally, it would be useful if students could discuss two or three arguments.
○ Conclusions and recommendations: what are the key final points that can be made and what suggestions are made for the future?

ENCOURAGING GCSE STUDENTS TO MAKE GOOD PRESENTATIONS

There are many vocational and non-vocational programmes that are directly relevant to citizenship. Perhaps the most direct link can be seen in social science AS and A level programmes. Review the specifications and examination papers of those courses in order to ensure you're engaged in the best work available for your students.

A good guide to GCSE and other courses has been written by Ralph Leighton and can be seen at www.citized.info. It's important to monitor the new developments that will be associated with the Tomlinson report to judge whether the profile citizenship education has is likely to rise or fall. It is possible that GCSE examinations will disappear over the next few years and be replaced in a massive overhaul.

It is also worth investigating the existence of activities that are examined in non-traditional ways: many of the tutorial programmes managed by schools (especially in the post-16 context) can be very useful indeed for citizenship education. It might also be possible to develop work around the activities (or, *some* of the activities!) that students get up to beyond school (for example, a range of community and political activities).

Learning from others

The IEA (International Association for the Evaluation of Educational Achievement) civic education study provides a rich source for those who wish to understand something of the issues that characterize citizenship education in more than 30 countries. The project was divided into two stages with the first part concerned with the review of curriculum initiatives, policy statements, textbooks, etc. in order to provide some context. The key publication from this part was: Torney-Purta *et al.* (1999).

Details of the second part (www2.hu-berlin.de/empir _bf/press.html)that involved more school-based work, including responses from young people, can be accessed through various routes including the website of the National Foundation for Educational Research (www.nfer.ac.uk).

Another survey that will be of interest is the QCA sponsored INCA study of 16 countries, again available through the NFER website.

Some impressive international work has been undertaken by Lynn Davies (no relation to me!) of Birmingham University. It is worth looking at journals such as *Comparative Education* for articles on key issues.

The Children's Identity and Citizenship in Europe network has published a number of books (edited by Alistair Ross) based on single nation studies and some comparative work.

It is not possible to summarize in a few lines the sort of work that is taking place across the USA, but Carole Hahn's chapter in Torney-Purta *et al.* (1999) is a great place to start. Young people are seen as 'becoming political'. But there have been complaints about the fraying of civic spirit by authors such as Putnam (his book titled 'Bowling Alone' is well worth a read), however, there's also a great deal of individual and group volunteering and a focus on controversial and diffuse initiatives such as character education. Probably the single best source for what is happening in this area can be found in the National Council for the Social Studies. The NCSS annual conference is a large-scale event that brings together teachers and academics from across the USA and beyond.

Other countries have been promoting citizenship education. It is worth having a look at the Discovering Democracy initiative from Australia (just type 'discovering democracy' into any good Internet search engine). Also the civic education syllabus from Ontario (see Evans *et al.* 2000). It is also very interesting to see how countries in transition are developing citizenship education, for example Hong Kong and Hungary.

Key reading:
Torney-Purta, J., Schwille, J. and Amadeo, J.-A. (1999) *Civic Education across countries: 24 national case studies from the IEA Civic Education Project*. Amsterdam: IAEEE.
Fouts, J. and Lee, W. O. (2004) *Citizenship Education*. Hong Kong: University of Hong Kong Press.
Evans, M., Slodovnick, M., Zoric, T. and Evans, R. (2000) *Citizenship: Issues and Action*. Toronto: Prentice Hall.
Putnam, R. (2000) *Bowling Alone: the collapse and revival of American community*. New York: Simon and Schuster.

THE NFER STUDY INTO CITIZENSHIP EDUCATION

The study, published in May 2004, suggests that schools need to review how they teach citizenship education. It also highlights that schools that have implemented citizenship successfully have taken a holistic and coherent approach to developing citizenship education in the curriculum, in the school as a community and in partnership with the wider community.

Other success factors include:

o a clear, coherent and broad understanding of what is meant by citizenship education;
o a supportive school ethos;
o support from senior management and a dedicated and enthusiastic coordinator – a 'citizenship champion';
o equal status and value accorded to citizenship alongside other subjects;
o recognition of the need for staff training and development;
o sufficient time and resources and a range of delivery approaches;
o active involvement of students in school activities.

The report recommends that:

o schools should adopt a holistic approach, encompassing not only moral and social dimensions but also political literacy and concern with public policy issues;
o policy makers need to adopt a broad, 'developmental' view of citizenship education that highlights growing signs of progress alongside deficiencies;
o recognition is required of the need for staff training and development.

To order the study *Making Citizenship Education Real. Citizenship Education Longitudinal Study Second Annual Report: First Longitudinal Survey* contact DfES Publications and quote the ISBN: 1844782220.

Taylor and Johnson (2002) completed some research and developed guidelines for practice (see also Idea 20 and Section 6). Only a few of their recommendations have been given below.

Status of the council:

○ display photos of council representatives;
○ give representatives a notice board;
○ give the council a budget;
○ allocate time for class feedback and discussions;
○ a member of the Senior Management Team should be a member of the council;
○ inform staff of decisions and developments;
○ liaise with governors.

Making the most of the council:

○ set clear achievable aims;
○ link the council to citizenship education (explain the process of elections; connect the council to the curriculum).

Concerning meetings:

○ decide the optimum frequency of meetings;
○ decide the optimum length of term of office to ensure as many as possible get a chance to become involved and there is sufficient time for councillors to learn and practise the role;
○ ensure optimum length of meetings;
○ involve administrative staff so there's an appropriate degree of assistance.

Concerning councillors:

○ explain matters carefully, especially to younger students;
○ arrange for ex-councillors to induct new councillors;
○ cultivate an ethos in which being a councillor is respected.

Concerning non-councillors:

o help councillors provide effective feedback;
o keep a record of decisions and ensure others get to know about them;
o when change takes place ensure that the idea is attributed to the class where it originated.

Key reading:
Taylor, M. J. and Johnson, R. (2002) *School Councils: their role in citizenship and personal and social education.* Slough: National Foundation for Educational Research.

The question for this particular review was: What is the impact of citizenship education on the provision of schooling? (See: http://eppi.ioe.ac.uk/EPPIWeb/home.aspx?&page=/reel/reviews.htm.) It was carried out in August 2004 and an overview of some of the findings is below (summarized from their website).

Learning and teaching:

o The quality of dialogue and discourse is central to learning in citizenship education.

o Transformative, dialogical and participatory pedagogies complement and sustain achievement rather than divert attention from it.

Curriculum construction and development:

o Dialogue and discourse are connected with learning about shared values, human rights and issues of justice and equality.

o Engagement of students in citizenship education requires educational experiences that are challenging, attainable and relevant to students' lives and narratives.

School ethos and context:

o Schools often restrict participation by students in shaping institutional practices but expect them to adhere to policies and this can be counter-productive to the core messages of citizenship education.

o A facilitative, conversational pedagogy may challenge existing power/authority structures.

Leadership and management:

o Strategies for consensual change have to be identified by and developed in educational leaders.

o A coherent whole-school strategy, including a community-owned values framework is a key part of leadership for citizenship education.

External relations and community:

o Contextual knowledge, and problem-based thinking can lead to (citizenship) engagement and action.

AN EPPI (EVIDENCE FOR POLICY AND PRACTICE INFORMATION) PROJECT

Teacher learning, knowledge and practice:

o Teachers require support to develop appropriate professional skills to engage in discourse and dialogue to facilitate citizenship education.
o Listening to the voice of the student leads to positive relationships, an atmosphere of trust and increases participation. It may require many teachers to 'let go of control'.
o Participative and democratic processes in school leadership require particular attitudes and skills on the part of teachers and students.

A paper by David Halpern, Peter John and Zoë Morris (*Journal of Education Policy* Volume 17 Number 2, pp. 217–28) reports the results of a survey of citizenship education practice in Hertfordshire carried out in June 2000. They wanted to know if the practice in schools was as negligible as conventional wisdom and existing research suggested. They found that:

- 8 per cent of schools claimed not to be doing anything at all;
- 17 per cent delivered citizenship as a discrete subject;
- most schools offered extra-curricular activities which contributed to citizenship education;
- 80 per cent of mainstream schools provided at least some coverage of most topics;
- just under 80 per cent of the mainstream schools designated someone to coordinate citizenship education;
- 32 per cent of schools thought citizenship education should be devised at the discretion of each school.

Overall, the findings conveyed the diversity of practices, and suggest a more autonomist conception of citizen education practice than that advocated by the English central government.

IDEA 95

BEFORE THE CITIZENSHIP ORDER

Professional development

DEVELOPING SUBJECT KNOWLEDGE

o **Review the demands relating to subject knowledge made by various government agencies.** What do the DfES, QCA, TTA and Ofsted expect of students? How does citizenship education fit (or not fit) with the most recent initiatives (e.g. KS3 strategy)? I am not suggesting that these points are learned or revered but they are important government guidelines and need to be regarded in a constructively critical manner.

o **Review demands on subject knowledge associated with examination boards.** What are the similarities and differences between AQA, Edexcel and OCR for citizenship? It will be important to review examination papers, mark schemes and additional guidance to markers rather than assuming that the board will really reward those areas that it asserts are important.

o **Create subject knowledge media folders.** Develop media folders classifying stories that relate to different areas of subject knowledge (the areas from the National Curriculum Citizenship Order could provide the key sections of the folder).

o **Encourage collaboration between colleagues so knowledge can be shared.** What can be gained from colleagues in other departments? Useful conversations can take place with colleagues in history, geography, science, etc. Their subject associations will provide guidance on citizenship that you might find useful.

o **Review published material.** Subject associations and other organizations are normally keen for reviews to be written of published material. If you can be accepted as a reviewer this will be interesting and enjoyable but also ensure that you are kept up to date with the latest publications.

o **Establish regular subject knowledge reviews.**
Once each year look again at your citizenship syllabus
and ask yourself what sort of knowledge have you
covered and what, in light of recent developments,
now needs updating?

o **What new reading is available?** In the review
sections of magazines such as *Prospect, New
Statesman, Spectator, New Yorker, The Times Literary
Supplement*, etc. new material is summarized and one
can easily and enjoyably learn about contemporary
issues.

We have moved on somewhat from the supposed radical days of the 1960s–1980s when teachers were accused by politicians, and the rather imaginative media, of being determined to force schools to become sites of radical action. That was never a realistic reflection of what was happening. Interestingly, it's possible that schools and teachers have become 'progressive' or 'liberal' in their use of language, dress codes and general expectations of young people, and, at the same time, in their pursuit of academic qualifications and adherence to centralized policies more 'conservative'.

Ask student teachers to think of three communities (e.g. the press and other media; parents; teachers of a subject other than citizenship) and their potential reaction to the following:

A student teacher is with an English class. A project has been organized on the nature of language. A serious point about the use of language in different communities is being developed. The class is being shown the afternoon's TV coverage of the 3.30pm horse race from Newmarket in order to analyse the language of the commentator, the bookmakers, the riders and owners. This is being done prior to an exploration of the sort of specialist language used by politicians. The head teacher unexpectedly brings a visitor to the classroom who is considering enrolling his child into the school. What reactions would you expect? Has anyone acted unprofessionally: if so, who, how and why?

A simpler activity would be to consider a list of key behaviours (dress, speech, arrival time, presentation of written work, prompt achievement of tasks, communication with colleagues, etc.) and discuss what would be regarded as professional behaviour in each context. Consider why certain judgements are being made in certain contexts. Is it normally the case, for example, that citizenship teachers are more casually dressed than others in the staff room? If so, does this matter? Are teachers expressing political views and if so how? Certain types of clothing are now banned in schools in France: is this justified? Should we ban the wearing of wedding rings given it can be viewed as an assertion of sexual identity?

Consider the following simple lesson plan:

o   establish aim;
o   undertake teaching activity;
o   assess school students;
o   establish new aim.

Now consider a real lesson. Can the features shown above be identified or not? If so, were those features used in the planning process in the same order as shown above?

Think about whether each of those elements could be used as a starting point. For example, an activity is generated not because it has a clear aim but rather because it is thought to be an interesting and enjoyable thing to do. Then start to work out if that activity could have a set of educational aims attached to it and what sort of assessment would be required. Now go further and question whether for citizenship the use of these features can ever be appropriate.

For some, citizenship is not to be taught in the same way as other lessons. It is possible to argue, by those who believe that citizenship is not the same as other subjects, that aims and assessment exercises are not to be considered at all when lessons are being planned. What do you think?

PLANNING LESSONS: WHAT STRUCTURES ARE BEST FOR CITIZENSHIP LESSONS?

CITIZENSHIP AND CLASS MANAGEMENT

A vast amount of material already exists to help teachers consider what needs to be done to manage classes and individuals effectively and appropriately. Citizenship, however, is thought by many to be more concerned with process than almost any other subject. The ways in which a teacher interacts with the class (as they promote a specific form of 'classroom climate') is said by some (see the reviews of research provided elsewhere in this book) to be a key feature of the citizenship teachers' work. What do you think about the sort of teacher behaviour shown below? Consider not just whether the teacher is an effective manager but, more precisely, what the class will be learning about citizenship if the teacher acts in this way.

A teacher stands very close to a student who is seated. There is direct eye contact. Explanations are being given by the teacher. The teacher makes a chopping motion with his hand as each point is made. [Possible response: the teacher is in charge; the student has to listen as the expert gives clear knowledge. There is a clear hierarchy in the class.]

A teacher stands next to the whiteboard while talking to the whole class. The teacher leans back to hold the edge of the board, moves from foot to foot and occasionally fiddles with the buttons on their jumper and with a pen. [Possible response: the teacher is unable to control the situation; is unsure and the class are being invited to seize power. This is not a democratic environment.]

A teacher goes to a school student who is seated at a desk. The teacher leans down by bending their knees. Eye contact takes place occasionally. Nodding occurs when the student speaks. [Possible response: some suggest that this shows an attempt by the teacher at collaboration; it could be simply manipulative, but there is an attempt to share power.]

Some more detailed guidance on assessment is available in Section 9. At this point I would like only to recommend a simple, but in my view highly effective, way of getting people to realize the nature of assessment. In a paper placed on the citizED website ('Post 14 citizenship examinations'; www. citized.info), Ralph Leighton advises the following as a way of developing understanding about assessment criteria. The following is written for a group of teachers (it could form the basis of a citizenship team meeting) but it is also possible for an individual to reflect on the meaning of assessment criteria.

○ Stage 1: One member of the group is asked to clap and the others are asked, in turn, to give a mark out of ten. As the group leader asks others to state the mark they award, they are also asked to explain how they arrived at this mark.

○ Stage 2: A second member of the group is asked to clap. Again, others are asked to award a mark out of ten. This time they are given headings to consider: 'volume', 'appropriateness', 'rhythm' and 'enthusiasm'. Again comments should be sought to clarify/justify the marks given.

○ Stage 3: A third member of the group is asked to clap. This time he or she is given a very clear context for the clapping, for example: 'You have attended a performance by your favourite musician. Show your reaction'. The group is given the same headings to consider as for Stage 2, this time with clear descriptions of what is meant by them written in clear view and explained.

1 Volume: The extent to which the volume of clapping meets the requirements of the task. (Therefore, not necessarily 'how loud'.)

2 Appropriateness: The extent to which the style is appropriate to the task, for example, assessment within context of concert, football stadium, talent show, etc.

PROFESSIONAL DEVELOPMENT AND ASSESSMENT OF CITIZENSHIP EDUCATION

3 Rhythm: The extent to which the rhythm meets the requirements of the task e.g. rapturous applause, sporting or national rhythms.

4 Enthusiasm: The extent to which levels of enthusiasm demonstrated meet the requirements of the task e.g. 'half-hearted' to reflect polite disappointment.

The person clapping is then asked to explain how they responded to the task, making reference to the given criteria. Then other members of the group are asked to give their responses.

Once this has been established it is possible to take one aspect of citizenship and suggest a framework for assessment. Social and moral responsibility could be tackled as perhaps the hardest of the areas and for more on this, p. 55 could provide some food for thought.